Other books by this author include:

I Stumbled across a Time Machine (Xulon Press)
The Government Stole My Time Machine (iUniverse)
Exit before Entering (Infinity Press)

EXPRESSIONS OF THE
LAST DAYS

JEFF PORTER

WESTBOW·
PRESS
A DIVISION OF THOMAS NELSON
& ZONDERVAN

WestBow Press books may be ordered through booksellers or by contacting:

WestBow Press
A Division of Thomas Nelson & Zondervan
1663 Liberty Drive
Bloomington, IN 47403
www.westbowpress.com
1 (866) 928-1240

ISBN: 978-1-4908-3254-8 (sc)
ISBN: 978-1-4908-3255-5 (hc)
ISBN: 978-1-4908-3253-1 (e)

Library of Congress Control Number: 2014905986

Printed in the United States of America.

WestBow Press rev. date: 05/15/2014

CONTENTS

Introduction...vii

1. Bubble, Bubble, Toil and Trouble 1

2. The Problem of Deception...................................... 12

3. What Is Apologetics? 35

4. What about the Cults?.. 44

5. The Church in Crisis... 60

6. The Approaching Judgment.................................... 99

7. King Kong, Gorgo, and the Blob............................. 107

8. Armageddon... 159

Suggested Reading List 165

INTRODUCTION

When I walk through a bookstore and see all the apocalyptic literature, not only Christian but also secular, I wonder if my writing will only clutter an already glutted market and therefore further confuse an already confused reading audience. However, I also have a burning desire to put forth a message that seems to be missing from the already existing books and magazines. I also believe that message is burning within the heart of God. I believe he desires so earnestly for Christians and non-Christians alike to know that message.

I do not believe God has given us all the timeless prophecies in the Old and New Testaments only to show us that he is God and he can see into the future and tell us about it. He has given us forewarnings of things to come so we will not be caught unaware and unsuspecting of the terrible troubles that are about to come upon this world. He has warned us so we can be prepared in heart, spirit, and mind to face these troubles and survive in the midst of them. We will not only to survive, barely breathing and shaking, but there is a victory even in the worst of times. We can turn toward his face and receive the peace, power, love, and grace we need to survive the coming awful days of tribulation that stands at our doorstep at this very hour.

As Christians, we should not be so deaf to this message or so assuming that we are caught with our defenses down and our shining armor on the ground. Jesus said in Luke 21:34 not to be caught unaware and let our hearts be weighed down with the cares of this life and drunkenness. They will upon us suddenly and as a snare, *for they will come upon all those who dwell upon the earth.* But pray that you will be found worthy to escape all these things to stand before him.

One of the most tragic things to come upon modern Christianity is a rise toward materialism and an over-concern for the cares of this life. Are we to assume that we are found worthy already to escape all these things? Or should we take a second look at ourselves and reevaluate whether we are ready—whether we have taken the time to study the Scriptures and to find their true meaning? Whatever conclusion you the reader come to or have already come to, we must all admit when it comes to the holiness and righteousness of God, there is always room for improvement.

I am by no means an expert on the subject of Bible prophecy or apologetics. I have, with the help of the Holy Spirit, studied the Bible and prophecy on my own over the years I have been a Christian. My idea in writing this book is not to badger my reading audience (which I am very grateful for) with my "right" opinions. Instead it is to inform you that the destiny of this desperate world is already mapped out. God, in his infinite wisdom, already knows the map from one end to the other. But the fact of the matter is that *we* are the most important elements of his plan. He cares for each one of us even though it may look like this world is about to come unglued.

Chapter 1

BUBBLE, BUBBLE, TOIL AND TROUBLE

A serious look at our troubled world shows it is obviously in turmoil, and it does not look like it's going to change for the better, at least not soon. What exactly is causing our trouble?

Well, in Matthew 24, Jesus spelled out many of the problems and troubles that would come upon this world right before his second return. That was two thousand years ago, yet his words describe our present situation in accurate and graphic detail.

Jesus' disciples came to him privately and asked him what the signs would be of his coming and the end of the world. Amazingly, he did not hesitate to give his most frightening and interesting account of the world's condition near the last days and the end of this era as we know it.

He started by saying we should beware of many false prophets and false teachers who would appear in Christ's name. He said they would deceive many. We certainly would not be at a loss to come up with good examples of false messiahs and false prophets in our generation. Some even started out as sincere and godly leaders but have ended up in tragedy—sometimes violent tragedy—for themselves and their followers.

I've heard many people ask how such a thing could happen in our supposedly enlightened and educated society. It happens for many reasons. One of the biggest reasons it happens is because we have become very strong in the knowledge of the world and very weak in the knowledge of God. We are not educated in the Bible, and we do not have a proper God-given understanding that comes from self-education and the prayer closet. In the past few decades, people in this country and many others have gotten caught up in a rush toward materialism. Seeking those things can only bring temporary satisfaction to the inner self. Our civilization seems only interested in money, sensual gratification, and power over men, which again can only bring that temporary satisfaction to the earthly self.

What happens next is easy to understand. Many people *do* become dissatisfied with the idea of just accumulating things and having the best of this and that. Frustration builds within them to break out and do something drastically different—perhaps something at the other end of the spectrum. Unfortunately, though, they do not always do the right thing. They are often desperately grasping at straws and are simply looking in the wrong place for that satisfaction.

Many—and I might say most—of these self-proclaimed messiahs come with a package of promises and hopes for people who are searching and thirsting for something more than their drab world has to offer. Materialism or the boring routine of their lives has left them so weary, empty, and dry that they are willing to try just about anything. Our new messiah, whoever he is, has come to offer them more. In fact, these people offer much more than anything or anyone could possibly give.

Sin and rebellion run fairly rampant in our streets, homes, and workplaces. People grow tired of the fear, insecurity, and craziness of it all. They begin to crave the love, security, and hope of their new leader. He is the symbol of the opposite life. In other words; he promises all the things human beings spiritually hunger for. He becomes their whole world and the culmination of their dreams of a better life and a hopeful future.

The next step for our Christ-like figure is to convince his followers or potential followers that he can indeed keep his promises. He does this in many ways, but one of the most important ways is through miracles, or supposed miracles, performed in the presence of his audience. Whether his miracles are real is not the point. The point is to make his followers *believe* they are real. This display of spiritual fireworks causes them to fall further and further into his grasp until there is little that will convince them otherwise.

Let's take a look at Matthew 24:24. Jesus said false prophets would come and show great signs and wonders. They would be so convincing that these miracles, signs, and wonders would deceive God's own people. But what shall become of those who are not believers? The prospect of such a question is frightening indeed.

3

I remember watching a television documentary in which a reporter was investigating a self-proclaimed messiah. He was able to trick people into believing he could turn the pages of a book from a distance or levitate objects from the floor. The reporter painstakingly exposed him as a cheap magician, a sleight-of-hand trickster who used his tactics to deceive his followers into believing he had developed his mind beyond normal abilities.

What really caught my attention was something the reporter said during his commentary toward the end of the program. He said the more people are convinced they cannot be deceived, the more easily they *are* deceived. In other words, when a man is convinced he is knowledgeable and enlightened in his own world of understanding and overlooks little of what passes his way, it is possible his *attitude* alone could cause him to overlook the most obvious flaw. If a man is convinced he knows best and is enlightened without God and is self-sufficient in what he has already learned, is it not possible that when something he has not encountered happens, the event could shake his foundation? It would be logical to assume, therefore, that the average man in today's materialistic society is ill-prepared to face the onslaught of such a spiritual event, especially one so earthshaking as to defy all sense of logical conformity to existing scientific reasoning and laws.

We now come to another subject that links to this problem of false prophets. New developments in our society's thinking have removed some barriers, such as materialistic science. Back in the fifties and early sixties, people were not so interested in much of anything the normal senses could not take in. In other words, if it could not be seen, heard, tasted, or felt, it could not logically exist. What has happened in the last few decades really staggers the imagination. The scientific world, as well as the rest of the world, has been opened to a whole new world of psychic phenomenon. Major universities have departments to study dreams, mental telepathy, astral projection, ghosts, and other phenomena. This new open-mindedness is amazing, considering the scientific community was so strongly against these things not so long ago. With another barrier out of the way, we can see that science, which once created an atmosphere of security, is no longer a strong barrier to this kind of deception. This is another reason for the amazing success of false prophets. We can also see science itself is searching for something beyond the everyday world.

Another reason for the success of false prophets is our natural, built-in need for love, security, attention, and I might add, social acceptance. Followers and potential followers are given the immediate gratification that comes from being part of the crowd. It is difficult to shake such a feeling, and it is one of the most devastating and enticing powers false prophets have at their disposal. Almost everyone has, at one time or another, felt left out, lost, or unloved. This is when we are the most vulnerable to a deception of this type. This kind of desperation and deception can not only drive one to worshipping a false hero, but it can also lead us to drugs, alcohol, perversion, or even suicide.

False prophets will often recommend drugs, alcohol, or illicit sex to open the mind or ease the pain of life. But the actual truth of the matter is that these things only serve to dull the senses and to further these prophets' plans to draw their followers into whatever they want. They will bring down built-in defenses and drag individuals deeper and deeper into the caves of engulfing darkness. Jesus gave this warning at least three times in Matthew 24 alone: Beware of false prophets and false Christs, because they are coming. Their lies and miracles are strong and enticing. See that you are not deceived or taken in by them. He was trying to convince us that we can be deceived if we are not properly warned and armed against it.

If Jesus emphasized something more than once, as he did here, then he really means what he says with the utmost seriousness and soberness. We ought to give it more careful consideration before we fly by it, saying, "It can't happen to me." The Lord himself said it can happen to you and me. This is exactly what he kept saying. This subject is extremely important, and I will refer to it time and again in this book. I will point out that when the Antichrist comes to power, the awful tidal wave of his lies and deceptions can and will catch most of the world with its defenses down.

Wars

In Matthew 24:6, Jesus said that we would begin to hear about wars and rumors of wars. There are at this moment many military conflicts taking place in different parts of the globe. The nations are in conflict over religion, territory, and conflicting governmental concepts. The atmosphere is stirred up by tensions and terrorists groups and warring factions who seek to gain control by way of violence, propaganda, and/or fear tactics. The subject of war has always been with us, so why bring it up now as one of the signs of the end? Because wars have increased beyond the usual level in the last few decades.

The weapons of war have and are changing and becoming more and more deadly as technology advances. I was in the army in the early seventies, and I can tell from personal observations that an all-out conventional war is really unthinkable. The area of combat in an all-out ground war would be so spread out and the battleground so saturated with heavy artillery and machine-gun fire that the average soldier would stand very little chance of surviving for more than a few days or weeks at the most. Certainly no one would come out unscathed in one way or another.

Natural Disasters

However, Jesus does not stop there in describing the world's condition in the last days. He goes on to say in verse 6 that all these things must come to pass but the end is not yet. In verse 7 he said that nation shall rise against nation and kingdom against kingdom. He also said that famines and pestilences (flies, mosquitoes, and frogs) would increase in diverse or different places.

Famines and pestilences have always been with us but seem more prevalent in the last few decades. When communism took over in Vietnam right after the war, hundreds and thousands of people were driven out for purely political reasons. We came to know these people as the boat people. Thousands of people starved to death or fled into greater dangers during this dreadful time. There have been uncountable famines all over the world over the last thirty years. Some attributed this to the futility of war and some to natural disasters. This problem of food shortages causes all sorts of other problems, such as the spread of disease and the demoralization of large numbers of people.

Earthquakes are usually accompanied by other problems, such as terrific tidal waves or erupting volcanoes. Mount St. Helens is a perfect example. Another memorable quake is a heavy one that leveled two cities in Japan just a few years ago. As the earth begins to reel toward the end, Jesus indicated these powerful quakes would begin to increase significantly. Does this mean we are in the last of the last days at this very moment?

What I would like to point out to the reader is that when we begin to see a major increase in earthquakes and natural disasters that are totally out of proportion, we should take heed of Scripture and be ready for the rest of Bible prophecy to begin to take place. I believe that what is important here is that we as Christians realize there are things happening in the world right now that are *leading up to the tribulation*. We need to recognize these things and stay active to fight against them, especially false doctrine and false prophets' attacks on the gospel. From my own observations, the church is very laid back in this area and needs to give it much more attention than it is now.

Violence

We as a nation are in trouble when it comes to crime and violence. It is increasingly popular to thumb our proverbial noses at the Bible, the laws of man, and even our own consciences. Need I point out statistics that should belong to the Ripley's Believe It or Not museum? According to FBI statistics, an unusual and violent crime is committed on the average every two seconds in some part of the United States.

Much of our problem with rampant sin comes from what we believe inside ourselves on a daily basis. Most people, if asked what they really believe about God, morality, or their general views on the world's condition, really couldn't come up with a strong answer. It's hard to see this if one has not truly sat down and pondered it, but it is what a person believes from the heart that motivates one's actions. Unfortunately, most folks don't really think about this and float along just accepting whatever the world tells them to believe. This is very dangerous, and this is also exactly why Satan is able to keep the world moving forward toward the tribulation and the final judgment of God. Most of the human race does not take the time to think about the way things are happening in the world and what they mean. The warning signs are everywhere yet are largely ignored, in some instances even by the church. This is a very important subject, though, and I will be referring to it in later chapters.

Television

Television is increasingly using sex and violence as a major part of entertainment. It is spewing out all sorts of information and propaganda in favor of the typical liberal view. It is teaching children to believe in magic and occult practices while it finds fault with the church. How many documentaries have you seen that are in favor of the Bible or the conservative doctrine of Christ? Most of the programs of this nature that explore the area of religion are very critical of this church or that preacher. Much of the criticism is based on the church's intake of money or the fact that the church can operate on a tax-free basis. Yet these same companies that attack the church are themselves multimillion-dollar conglomerates and base their income on constantly bombarding the American mind with endless and sometimes ridiculous commercials they produce. (I wouldn't know what to do if I had dandruff.)

I think television is one of the greatest spiritual battlegrounds of our day. If one were to take a closer look, one would notice that forces are at work in both subtle and overt ways. It is by far the most popular medium of powerful persuasion of masses of people. It should be used with the greatest of care and responsibility, yet it is being used for the pull of the almighty dollar in so many ways. Liberals say that all censorship should be removed and that if we are offended, we can turn it off. Yet I am concerned with the fact that TV has become such a habit for millions of people that just turning it off is not really an option. It has become such a part of our daily lives, yet we seem to have so little control over what is aired. We have become so absorbed in what we are watching that we may not realize the seduction and power it may have over us. Slowly but surely it has become more openly immoral and violent. As television producers look for new and better ways to hold their audiences captive, they seem to think storylines are no longer viable, and plots are replaced with mindless eroticism and blood. Perhaps we should give this subject greater consideration than we have in the past.

I have only touched on some of the problems our nation and our world are facing in our modern times. Jesus said in Matthew 24:8 that these things are only the beginning of sorrows. If these things are only the beginning of what will take place in the future, what should we be studying to keep ourselves safe from the deceptions of the world? This is the subject of discussion in the rest of the chapters. I will also include some lessons about what happens in the very end and the final judgment of God on our world.

Chapter 2

THE PROBLEM OF DECEPTION

> In whom the god of this world hath blinded the
> minds of them which believe not, lest the light of
> the glorious gospel of Christ, who is the image of
> God, should shine unto them. (2 Cor. 4:4)

The Bible speaks of Satan as being the *god* of this world in a very peculiar way in this verse. It is, of course, not saying that the Devil has the same power and authority over the universe as God himself. It is stating the fact that the unbelieving world gives their allegiance to him and doesn't realize they are born into a state of darkness and are in desperate need of a heart conversion to be born again spiritually into the kingdom of God. They need to change their allegiance from the kingdom of darkness to the kingdom of light to spend eternity in the right place. A truly born-again Christian who has already come to the light from darkness can understand this verse perfectly, but the world, reeling in darkness, does not.

As all honest Christians know, deception is Satan's most-used and most-powerful weapon against the children of God and the unbelieving world. Now let's take a step back and look at the big picture. Let's ask a kind of scary question. What could Satan do to move the church and the unbelieving world further away from the truth of the gospel and their own consciences? What would he have to do to remove all barriers of conscience and introduce a world with a majority of people devoid of God and marching toward moral decay and chaos?

Well, as we have already stated, the unbelieving world is already living in a static or motionless darkness. The nonbeliever is unaware of this condition for the most part and is also unaware of the redeeming power of the cross or the benefits of knowing the Lord Jesus Christ on a personal basis. The nonbeliever is already deceived to a major degree in the most important area of life. Many nonbelievers have a basic understanding of right and wrong in certain areas. The average non-Christian (noncriminal) is basically moral in that he or she has learned to follow the laws of the land, does not commit major crimes, and knows the basic elements of moral behavior, such as the evils of lying, cheating, stealing, and so on. These basics are taught to us from the beginning by our parents and society but are virtually unknown until taught by an outside source. But it is Satan's plan to remove those barriers at some point and inflict the world with moral chaos to rebel against God's plan for peace and love.

Politically Correct

How does he do this? There is a term that researchers and theologians have used for a long time to describe the removal of morals and conscience from our society. It is a word called *relativity.* This is a word that covers a lot of territory. It simply means there is no difference between right and wrong. In our modern world, we use the term *politically correct.* This is certainly not a new concept. Satan has been using it since the fall of Adam and Eve in the garden of Eden, and he will no doubt continue to use it as his greatest weapon until the end.

American universities and other institutions of learning fell prey to it a long time ago. Professors pronounce that one must decide within oneself what is right and wrong, and whatever one decides inside one's own heart is correct for that person. The late Keith Green (a Christian musician) wrote a song a few years ago called "Satan's Boast." In it Satan boasts that his job keeps getting easier as day slips into day. Satan says that he used to have to sneak around, but now they just open up their doors. He says that the magazines and newspapers now print every word he says. It makes us wonder how Satan could accomplish what would be a very difficult task—the task of introducing bold-faced lies to the human race so they will never suspect and will walk right into darkness without even questioning themselves or the reasons behind their actions.

His plan is very simple on one level and very complex on another. The simple part of the plan is that he must introduce his lies slowly, bit by bit in small pieces so the world doesn't choke on it and spit it out. He must introduce his ideas of giving up morality and intellect at the same time, and this requires that he get at the intellectuals or the brains of the world first and let the darkness slowly filter down to the rest of the world like slow-sifting of sands through a gigantic hour glass. So how does he do that? Very simply, he appeals to the basic desires of the human race. An intellectual person has wants and desires like any other human being. If this person desires to sin and can find a way to make it seem right, then the plan can be set in motion without a lot of difficulty.

Somewhere down the line, a once-moral and -ethical college began publishing books that rationalize immoral behavior in a most subtle way: by undermining the basics of the Bible and introducing a *new* way of looking at Scripture from a more "open-minded" point of view. Eventually that kind of thinking spreads out to the rest of the world, and slowly—over decades and even centuries—the barriers to sin are removed until most of the world views the Bible as some ancient, outdated, irrelevant book of myths that only some simple-minded, Bible-thumping country bumpkin would take seriously. I have talked to nonbelievers who have actually come right out and said that atheists are just naturally more intelligent, more refined, and better educated than Bible-believing Christians. This is the normal worldview of many intellectuals of our day.

Much of our modern-day thinking comes from the Greek civilization. I can't sit back and say all of it is all bad, because not all of it is. Much good has come from the way the Greeks handled things as far as philosophy and science are concerned. Much of our progress in science, medicine, and technology can be credited to the Greeks, and rightfully so. The Greek way of thinking brought in much of our understanding of experimentation and logic in mathematics to bring about the powerful technology we use today to make life quite a bit easier than it was in ancient times.

We are all glad that here in America we enjoy all of the benefits of advanced medicine and electronics. "For the Jews require a sign; and the Greeks seek after wisdom" (1 Cor. 1:22). But there is another dimension to life that some folks in science and philosophy have conveniently left out: the power of the cross and the redeeming grace of Christ. First Corinthians 1:23 says, "But we preach Christ crucified, unto the Jews a stumbling block, and unto the Greeks foolishness."

First of all the Bible, cannot be understood by pure logical reasoning and scientific investigation because it contains the wisdom of a being that is beyond our human understanding. To put it in more scientific terms, God is quite beyond our dimension or our space-time continuum. Therefore we cannot find him by intellectualizing our way to him.

This can be done up to a point simply because there is a lot of evidence in archeology, philosophy, and even astronomy to support the claims of the Bible as God's Word. A scientific law goes into effect because there is enough evidence to support its claim to reality. There is enough evidence in our day to make the Bible as historically accurate as any other historical document on the face of the earth. In fact, I would venture to say there is more evidence in favor of the Bible than *any other* book or document in the world.

But scholars who are hostile toward Christianity and the Bible also make the claim that the Christian belief system can be thrown out because of miracles. Miracles cannot be proven, so therefore the Bible cannot be proven. My answer to that is if the

Bible can be shown to be historically accurate, then why would the miracles become a myth? I would think, though, that since the study of astrophysics has shown us through the study of quantum physics (the study of tiny particles) that the universe is not as we once thought, most educated men would realize that miracles are certainly possible.

Satan has also introduced the idea that religion is the opiate of the people, as Carl Marx once stated. In other words, people use religion or some mystical belief system to rely upon to ease the pain and insecurity of both life and death. He is trying to put forth the idea that the more intellectual or educated man should rise above this mystical insecurity of life and face reality in a more suitable and logical manner and in so doing conquer life's problems with practical solutions rather than mythical methods that don't work.

But in the midst of this kind of thinking, the unbelieving world has left out the most important piece of the puzzle. This is the problem of sin. If sin hasn't caused all of the woes and suffering of the world, then what *has caused it?* The Bible is the only book that comes forward with an answer to the problem of lawlessness, and that is through that little word *grace.* We are saved from the eternal consequences of sin by grace or by simply believing in the person of Jesus Christ and his death upon the cross—not by intellectualizing but simply by believing. If we could be saved by intellectualizing, only intellectuals could be saved. But God made a plan that could reach even the slowest thinkers of the human race. God's method is quite simple and easy. All other belief systems are based on works. A person must climb up to

God if the way is made by working. But by simply believing, a person can be saved instantly, hassle free, a concept many scholars can't go along with.

Not only does "political correctness" or "relativity" have to do with science and philosophy, but it also cuts across religious barriers. Today most of the world has caught on to the idea that all religions are acceptable as long as one is loving and sincere in what one believes. Folks in every walk of life and in every level of society believe this to be true. This relativeness says that all religions are equal in what they believe because all religions are based on mysticism rather than scientific proof. It is therefore left up to the individual to decide since myths are unprovable. *But Jesus said in John 14:6,* "I am the way, the truth, and the life. No man comes unto the father but by me."

In many conversations with religious people and nonreligious people, I have been told that to believe John 14:6 is to be very narrow minded and bigoted. I am therefore labeled as a "fundamentalist" and a very opinionated one at that. But if we really think about it, all of the laws governing nature are very strict and narrow. If a brick is released from the top of a building, it can only fall one way. And this is true of most everything else concerning the way the world works.

Christians make the claim that there is only one spiritual book that truly proclaims the pure truth of God. But if there is only one God, how can all religions be true? Not all religions agree with each other on who and what God is. By the pure process of elimination, only one of the thousands could be true, and the rest must be thrown out. To say that all religions believe the same thing is total nonsense. Anyone who has looked at or read different religious material or listened to different speakers knows that there is a wide space between what religions believe. A person is better off to believe one or none of them rather than trying to embrace them all. But as many folks who have come to know Jesus as their Lord and Savior have found out, there is a spiritual hunger within us all that must be satisfied. To quote an old cliché, "A person who believes in nothing will fall for anything."

The fallout from political correctness has already caused terrible damage to our civilization, especially in the United States. The moral climate of our society is incredibly bad. I have already stated that crime and violence are climbing to terrific heights. Unbelievable crimes, such as school shootings and serial killings, are literally tearing our nation apart.

We are facing the problems of sexual freedom too. The problems associated with free sex are of course babies born out of wedlock and sexually transmitted diseases. Then there is the problem of drugs and alcohol taking its tremendous toll. I remember getting into a debate in technical school with some young women over some of these issues a few years ago. They were asking the question, "What's wrong with free sex? We can't tell kids just not to have sex. That's just not practical."

I finally raised my hand and said, "We have had this attitude that free sex and drugs should be allowed and practiced since at least the nineteen-sixties in America. Now we are facing the super-problems today because of it. What good has this liberal point of view done for us? I mean, if an idea has made life better for us, I'm all in favor of it. But what good has it done to believe this freedom stuff?" No one came up with an answer.

Evolution

Another concept Satan has introduced to the world for moral chaos is evolution. The thing that's weird about evolution is that you never hear anything about the creation side of the argument. Every time a documentary comes on TV, they always talk about evolution as if were absolute fact. As a matter of fact, it is not.

According to the theory of evolution, all forms of life on earth have developed from a single living cell. Then, over a period of billions of years, this cell changed into higher and different life forms until we have all the animals, plants, birds, and finally humans that are living today.

But there are many problems with this idea. First, there don't seem to by any intermediate life forms found in the fossil record. Over the vast stretch of time that evolution has supposed to have taken place, there would have to be billions of the in-between life forms molded into the rocks. Almost no evidence at all has been found in the rocks to verify Darwin's theory.

Let me make this more understandable. If we take a look at ants and look as far back in the fossil record as we can and then find the oldest possible ant that is etched into the rocks, we find that he is just the same old ant. He hasn't changed over those billions of years. The same is true of tigers, bats, and whales. They all show up in the rocks fully formed right from the beginning, without any evidence of an ancestor. *This holds true throughout the fossil record.* How could this be when the theory of evolution itself says that there must be billions of these intermediate creatures in the rocks? Scientists have tried to back up evolution with computer models showing that since there are similarities in DNA, evolution could have taken place. But if evolution doesn't show up in the fossil record, then computer models cannot change this fact.

Another problem with the theory is that you cannot crossbreed different kinds of animals in the present. In other words, you cannot cross a rhino with an elephant and get a relephant. Most of the time when this has been tried, the fetus won't even develop or it immediately dies. This causes many problems because the evolution model won't work if lower life forms cannot become higher life forms.

As a matter of fact, this is the next question. There should be massive evidence of evolution in the present. If evolution is continuing, then there should be half-men, half-apes walking around today? Billions of different intermediate creatures should be alive today all over the world. Where are they?

Dinosaurs

I also want to mention briefly the subject of dinosaurs and how they fit into biblical history. Thanks to television and magazines, most of us have come to think the study of dinosaurs can't fit with the context of the Bible. If one believes in evolution, I suppose this statement may be true. However, many statements from scientists about evolution are in error, so might their concepts of where the dinosaurs fit in be in error too?

From a quick look at the fossil record, again we do not find the intermediates for dinosaurs either. The fossil record is exactly as it should be if dinosaurs were simply created of God. But every time someone talks about dinosaurs in a museum, on television, or any other media, evolution is inserted with the dinosaurs as if it were an absolute fact that they evolved from the past. Why is this true when the evidence is quite to the contrary? Why is this information kept from the general public? Good question!

Some of us are skeptical of the most recent theories of how the dinosaurs died too. The most recent and most popular speculation says that a giant meteor plunged into the earth billions of years ago and spread ash into the earth's atmosphere. This in turn changed the climate and feeding habits of the animals and plants and eventually killed the dinosaurs. My question is, how did anything else survive?

There have been other theories ranging from the ridiculous to the outrageous. One such strange theory suggests that they died from constipation. What a way to go! There is no doubt in taking a look at the fossil record that many species of plants and animals have lived and died on the earth. So what's the big deal about the dinosaurs? I guess it's just the fact that dinosaurs are so huge and mysterious. The author will agree that dinosaurs are interesting indeed, but no reason really has been found to put them in conflict with the Bible.

I have heard folks say that the dinosaurs are not mentioned in the Bible. This would seem to be a problem from first glance. We, after all, seldom touch on such a subject in a typical Sunday school class. And it's true that the word *dinosaur* does not appear in the Bible. True, but the word *dinosaur* was not invented until much later after the Bible was written. However, we do find a strange creature or two in the book of Job in the Old Testament.

> Behold now behemoth, which I made with thee; he eateth grass as an ox. Lo now, his strength is in his loins, and his force is in the navel of his belly. He moveth his tail like a cedar: the sinews of his stones are wrapped together. His bones as strong as pieces of brass; his bones are like bars of iron. He is the chief of the ways of God: He that made him can make his sword to approach unto him. Surely the mountains bring him forth food where all the beasts of the field play. He lieth under the shady trees, in the covert of the reed, and fens. The shady trees cover him with their shadow; the willows of the brook compass him about. Behold, he drinketh up a river, and hasteth not: he trusteth that he can draw up Jordan into his mouth. He taketh it with his eyes: his nose pierceth through snares. (Job 40:15–24)

The other comes from Job 41. I haven't put that entire chapter here, so I recommend that you read it yourself. It's fascinating reading.

> Canst thou draw out Leviathan with an hook? Or his tongue with a cord which thou lettest down? ... Canst thou put an hook into his nose? Or bore his jaw through with a thorn? Will he make many supplications unto thee? Will he speak soft words unto thee? Will he make a covenant with thee? Wilt thou take him for a servant forever? ... His scales are his pride, shut up together as with a close seal. One is so near to another that no air can come between them. They are joined one to another; they stick together, that they cannot be sundered. By his neesings a light doth shine, and his eyes are like the eyelids of the morning. Out of his mouth go burning lamps, and sparks of fire leap out. Out of his nostrils goeth smoke, as out of a seething pot or caldron. (Job 40:1, 3–4, 15–20)

What's fascinating about the Leviathan is that it seems to breathe fire. The Creation Research Institute points out that a little bug called the bombardier beetle shoots fire and sparks from out of its rear. Yes, I said that right. It shoots hot sparks from out of its hind part (hot soup beans?) by shooting two chemicals together. This is the way most chemical rockets work today. When those two chemicals come together, they ignite because of their chemical makeup and properties. We could all get a bang out of this. The beetle does this to protect itself from predators. With all of the legends of fire-breathing dragons, is it possible that some of these legends may be true?

The Age of the Universe?

There has been much debate in the religious and nonreligious world about the age of the universe and the earth. The debate is inflamed by the fact that evolution requires millions of years for intermediate life forms to develop. Adding to the difficulty is the problem that radiometric dating methods have been found to be flawed. Carbon 14, for instance, requires that the amount of radioactive carbon in the earth's atmosphere remain constant over that vast stretch of time. More improved methods are being tested all the time, but the greatest difficulty lies in the fact that there is no real starting point to begin with. I wouldn't be surprised if all of these methods were found to be flawed in the future.

Astronomers have maintained for years that the universe must be billions of years old because of the vast distances in space and the amount of time it takes for the light from stars and galaxies to reach us. Some of these galaxies are billions of light-years (how far light travels in one year) from earth. Even at the speed of light (186,282 m/s), it would take billions of years for this light to reach us. However, recent discoveries have found that matter bends time and space and may therefore interfere with those time calculations. It may also be possible that God created the whole universe with a certain amount of age, just as he did with Adam and Eve in the garden of Eden. The debate, however, will probably continue until time stops because it may be just about impossible to unravel this riddle.

The Big Bang

We have all heard of the big bang theory, and it is quite interesting. The popular author and scientist Steven Hawking wrote a book a few years ago entitled *A Brief History of Time*, which did a great job of trying to explain this theory. Basically it says that the universe once existed in an area no bigger than a thimble or a baseball. Then it exploded and began to expand into what we have today.

This theory came about for a couple of reasons. First, because strange particles have been found coming from outer space that do not act as they are supposed to. As a matter of fact, they are so strange that scientists have separated the study from normal physics to a thing called quantum physics so the two wouldn't get confused. These particles are found on a subatomic level (smaller than atoms) and have been found to disappear and reappear and so on. The study of quantum physics has changed the very core of science in many ways and brought about some new discoveries and advancements. It has also opened up a whole new avenue of thought and brought in the idea of alternate or multiple universes. The big bang theory can be thought of as a possibility because this makes our universe possibly the end result of other universes creating each other. This is supposedly where we got the baseball-size object that started our universe to begin with.

Christians often think of the big bang as against God and creation, but many astronomers and astrophysicists are talking about intelligent design or a Creator (but are staying neutral as far as what religion might be right) because of the complication of a beginning.

Scientists also consider the big bang because the galaxies are moving away from each other and very fast. In this way, we can see that the universe as far as the masses contained in it is expanding. But it is really unknown as to why this is happening. Any honest scientist will tell you that the big bang is only the best theory they can come up with right now. But if the universe is moving, then something had to set it in motion. If we keep regressing back and asking where this and that came from (known as infinite regression), then we just keep coming back to God as the beginning of it all. A good portion of science, however, is more in favor of God than against. I find that to be really good news.

The Universe Is Winding Down

There is also another problem with a thing called the second law of thermodynamics. This law simply states that the universe is cooling. It is therefore going from a higher state to a lower state rather than the other way around. If you park a new car out in front of your house and just leave it there for many years, it is going to rust and fall apart. It will not get newer as time goes on. It will get old and eventually deteriorate into dust.

This does not fit with the theory of evolution because according to the theory, all life forms must go from a lower state to a higher one. It also means that the universe is spiraling down toward destruction rather than going up toward a better newer state of affairs. This is much in favor of creation because it shows that the universe could not have created itself and made all of the solar systems and galaxies by accident. Since it is cooling, it must have started at a higher state and is stepping down rather than the other way around.

Evolution Important?

Why is this issue of evolution versus creation so important? For good reasons. First and most obvious is because the theory gets in the way of the Genesis account of creation. If the universe created itself from nothing, then there is no need for God. As we can see, though, from just a little bit of reading and research anyone can find out that evolution has major problems without even comparing it to any creation material.

It is obvious, too, that those who want to skirt the issue of the existence of God must find a way around the idea of his first creating the universe. The study of astrophysics has attempted to do this, but after a period of years, many scientists are coming to the conclusion that the universe must have been created. They call it "intelligent design" and do not attempt to point toward any particular religion as the source, but nevertheless they see the hand of some higher power at work out there. This is very encouraging because it shows a greater open-mindedness than was before found in scientific circles.

By getting God and creation out of the picture, we can see another major problem with this concept. It is going to have a major impact on people's thinking and begin to remove moral values. Evolution in its own way is its own religion and the opiate of the people in reverse. If left unchecked, the awesomeness, beauty, and complexity of God's creation would speak for itself. It would be a strong barrier to keeping the majority of the earth's population in darkness.

Without evolution, the human race would simply look around at their breathtaking world and see it as the result of God's magnificent power of creation and praise him for it. But now that scientists and philosophers have painted a different picture, people don't see nature in that light of beautiful creation. They see it as a chain of accidents brought on by that ever-present and all-knowing concept called chance. It follows logically, therefore, that people would automatically begin to give in their basic human desires and lower their moral values. As a matter of fact, they begin to take on a whole new worldview that is much more distant and separated from our original Creator and that helps keep mankind in a perpetual state of ignorance and rebellion.

Most folks in the average world apart from the scientific world know very little about the details of the theory of evolution. Much of this has to do with the progress of science and technology. Since science has made so much progress over time and has changed our world so much for the better, most folks simply trust it and do not check it out for themselves.

One of the problems here is that science and philosophy have indeed done great things for our world and should be commended for these great achievements. But science, like all other institutions, is built and maintained by flawed human beings. And as we are all aware, flawed human beings make mistakes. In this case, human beings have allowed themselves to be manipulated by the unseen forces of darkness to trick our world into believing that God can be removed from the equation. But if God is removed from the equation, then the moral fabric of society is ripped apart, and it becomes riddled with heavy problems. The theory of evolution is therefore sawing off the very branch we are sitting on.

More than likely evolution will play a major role in the events leading up to the last days and during the times of the great tribulation. People will probably be more convinced that we are the product of accidental gradual change as time progresses toward the end. Satan will be able to latch on to this idea and explain to the world that we are going into a new era of our advancement.

The book of Revelation says that because the world will be worshipping the antichrist, God's judgment will be most severe. Satan will have to find some way outside of the Bible to explain what is happening to the world. The earth will experience unprecedented storms, upheavals in nature, wars, and persecutions. To combat the Bible's explanation of what's happening and to quell the fear of an angry almighty God, he will have to introduce the idea that because the human race is going through a change and feeling the effects of that change, we are therefore experiencing great upheaval. More than likely, he will say that since the human race is advancing to a higher state of mind and spirit. The old (outdated Christianity) must be thrown out and the new (occult beliefs) ushered in.

I would venture to say further that this is a subject of great importance to us today as Christians. The New Age movement, with its heavy beliefs in occult practices and witchcraft, is nothing to be ignored. It poses a great threat to the Christian belief system as it now stands, and it will more than likely succeed in causing great deal of damage to the world in the future.

The Occult

Those who have been involved in the occult and later been converted to Christ know how the systems of witchcraft and sorcery work. If a person appears to have psychic powers and can move objects across the floor, read minds, do astral projection, or any number of occult practices, it is with the help of demons. As the world reels toward the end and God's final judgment, people will get so caught up in worshipping the antichrist and believing his fanciful dreams that they will begin to acquire occultic powers. With the help of Satan's followers (the demons), they will be able to achieve a certain amount of success with these powers and be able to use them to manipulate their world up to a point. Most likely they will believe this is the end result of the evolutionary process, a clever but very nasty and terrible deception Satan very carefully conjured up over thousands of years just for the final climax of the earth's last chapter.

I also think that renewed interest in the UFO phenomenon is playing a major role in moving us toward the end. It is fascinating to think that we could be visited by beings from other worlds in outer space. This is another concept that is not necessarily all bad in that no one knows the complete answer as to whether there is life on other planets in the universe. But the antichrist may use this curiosity about outer space to make people think he is possibly an advanced being from another planet. Much of science fiction is devoted to the belief that we have been planted here by beings from another, much more advanced civilization. As time goes on and sinister plans unfold, Satan could make this idea become a common belief.

Cook Slowly over Small Flame

It has been said that if you put a frog in a pan, put him on a burner, and slowly turn up the fire, he will never realize he is being cooked. This is the way evil concepts are introduced into the world by the forces of darkness. At first the world is shocked by the idea of immoral actions. Over a long period of time, though, it begins to think that these things are a normal part of life, and eventually people even begin to fight for the right of these immoral concepts to be expressed. Anyone who opposes these new, more "open-minded" immoral actions and ideas is labeled as narrow-minded.

Once the big snowball of immorality gets a lot of snow on it and a lot of momentum, it's very hard to stop. That's why it's important to realize that we as Christians need to be aware of these things long before the book of Revelation opens and the terrible judgment of God begins. If we understand these concepts, it's much easier to reach the unsaved. This will allow us a much better, more-educated approach rather than just trying to beat folks over the head with a big black Bible. In a way, we must use the same strategy as the forces of darkness and introduce some of these concepts slowly so the unsaved mind can accept them. Otherwise they will most certainly choke and spit them out.

I am convinced that the personal evangelism of the individual Christian is the most important and key element to fighting evil and unbelief, especially in America. I am reminded of the story of a man who went to the doctor because of some pain he was feeling. When the doctor did an examination, he found the man to have some pockets of cancer in his system. The doctor decided that he didn't want to hurt the man's feelings, so he decided not to tell the patient there was anything wrong. Of course, eventually the man died from the cancer. Had the doctor told the man that he had cancer and risked offending or hurting him, he might have been able to prescribe some course of action to save his life. But he decided to take the easy road and shirk the responsibility of informing him of the problem or proposing possible solutions.

It may not always be possible to persuade folks that Jesus Christ and his Word are the answer in this world and in the next. But as God leads us forward in our work places and schools, it's important that we realize that there are folks around us who are on the wrong path and in need of our love and attention to get them on the right path. In order to do this, we need a stronger understanding of God's Word and his direction to any knowledge that would help us win souls for him. If God would happen to lead you to a person who is open and searching for truth, would you be able to reach into your bag of knowledge and help him or her come to a realization of Christ Jesus as his or her Savior? If not, would you be willing to dig and do some work and research to find an answer for that person? Perhaps Christians need answers for themselves too. That is the subject of my next chapter. How might we conduct this search?

Chapter 3

WHAT IS APOLOGETICS?

The word *apologetics* comes from the Greek word *apologia,* which means defense. You may ask, "Defense of what?" Well, an apologist might defend anything. There are Mormon apologists and atheist apologists. It all just depends on what you want to defend. In our case, we want to defend the Christian faith and the Christian point of view. Of course, in this arena too we are talking (hopefully) about the intellectual battlefield. If you were to begin a conversation about Christ, someone listening nearby may say that your statements about Christ are invalid because the Bible is not historically accurate. Then you might come up with some kind of evidence to support your claim that Jesus was indeed a real person in history and really did perform the miracles the Bible claims he did. At this point, you are supporting the Bible through the use of apologetics. Hopefully you are also doing this in a kind and loving way (but just do the best you can and pray as you go). You are then defending your Christian faith and becoming an apologist.

As you might have guessed, though, apologetics covers a much wider field than intellectual debate (or polemics, if you want to us a fancier word). It studies any scientific evidence that might support the Christian belief system. It would cover subjects such as evolution versus creation, astronomy or astrophysics, archeology, anthropology, paleontology, and so forth. Any information you can get your hands on and your head into that works in that particular situation will become very useful in dealing with your unsaved friends, coworkers, schoolmates, stubborn relatives, or kids. (Caution with teenagers—they are too smart.)

Apologetics also covers the very large field of the cults. This would include a very long list but to name a few: Mormons, Watchtower (Jehovah Witnesses), Hare Krishna, the Moonies, UFO cults, David Koresh, Jim Jones, the word of faith movement (found inside the Christian church), strange prophetic movements, and on the list goes. The apologist must look into these belief systems, gather a complete notebook or file on the particular subject, and proceed to study it and compare the claims and beliefs of this system to the Word of God. If it doesn't agree with the Bible, then it is considered false. At this point, it needs to be exposed as such and other folks warned of the dangers and damages it may pose to the church or the unsaved.

Apologetics in History

Since the very beginning, the Christian church has faced these sometimes-monumental challenges. Intellectual attacks and the rise of cults against the Christian faith are nothing new. We can always say, though, that God has been faithful in raising up apologists in various forms and different degrees to put out these raging fires of unbelief throughout history. There is mention of the Gnostics, who claimed a belief in Jesus but had all sorts of ridiculous beliefs surrounding the Christian doctrine, such as the belief that the body in itself was pure evil. When a Christian speaks of the flesh, we are talking about a sinful attitude, not a physical or tangible attribute (person, place, or thing) in the physical world. Finding a philosophical, spiritual, or scientific defense that works is the good work of a fine Christian working to find better and more effective ways to win souls because that is what Christian apologetics is all about—*winning souls.* It is not necessarily about winning arguments. But if an argument has to be won (for whatever reason) to win a soul, then the Christian could proceed with the powerful tools he has acquired to do just that.

Hostility

There is much hostility toward apologetics from within and without the church. Many Christians seem to think that defending the gospel with scientific proofs, logical arguments, or philosophy is invalid or just plain wrong for several reasons. The first is that they simply don't understand it. Much false teaching and many false doctrines have flooded Christianity in the past fifty years claiming that we are to preach only the Bible to folks and not to go too far in defending it because this may cause a conflict and offend the unsaved. Jude 3 refutes this idea of being soft and peaceful when it says that we are to contend earnestly for the gospel.

I think the confusion also comes from the belief that Jesus and the apostles were always nicey-nice and never said anything that offended anyone. But a quick and closer look at Scripture reveals quite a different picture than some folks are painting these days. Jesus soundly rebuked the scribes and Pharisees on several occasions and even told them they were like open graves. He said they looked fine on the outside, but on the inside, they were ravening wolves. Paul quoted the Old Testament and was very educated in Scripture when he defended Jesus and his teachings. Many times he did not mince words and was very straightforward in his arguments in favor of Scripture. Paul said that in his travels he was in danger of false brethren as well as thieves, raging rivers, and nasty people.

Much of this hostility seems to come from the Word of Faith movement (false teachings mostly from television) teaching Christians to lay down their spiritual weapons (the Word of God) and lay down their thinking caps (check brains here) and take up the idea that critical thinking and logical reasoning are out. Some Word of Faith teachers actually come right out and say that we are not supposed to think as Christians; we are supposed to act on faith only and revelations from God through prayer and personal words from God or new visions or dreams that he gives to us throughout our Christian life.

I believe wholeheartedly in visions and revelations from the Lord. I also believe in the power of the Holy Spirit in our lives and our hearts to give us encouragement and guidance. But as the days grow darker and the last days predicted in the Bible grow closer, I also believe we must become more cautious than ever before. *We must test the spirits through prayer and Bible reading. We must test what Christian leaders and teachers preach and write against the Word of God* (Acts 17:11). If they don't pass the acid test of God's Word, then they must not be respected and then exposed before they can do any more harm.

I was hostile toward the study of apologetics early on in my Christian walk. (I got saved in early May of 1978.) I was caught up in several false doctrines and was living a life of roaming the country with a Native American friend. There were times when I would go home to my parents to rest, though, and I would come into contact with an old buddy I knew from as far back as seventh grade. He had heard of my conversion to Christ from atheism, but he had also heard of my venture into false doctrines. He tried for several years to get me interested in apologetics and to read material that might educate me away from the harmful doctrines I believed.

Finally, one day I quit the streets, got a job, and started settling into a normal Christian life. The Lord had already set me free from many of my former beliefs, but I was still heavy into the Book of Mormon and the teachings of Don Juan. My friend handed me a book called *Who Really Wrote the Book of Mormon?* As I began reading it, I felt as though someone were stabbing me in the chest with little fiery darts. My friend also gave me a couple of tapes, which were lectures by the late Walter Martin (then living). I didn't like them too much then because I thought people like him were just trying to *intellectualize* the faith and therefore watering down the Spirit. Later on God set me free from the teachings of Don Juan through a dream (which I will

39

explain later). That is when I discovered the severe dangers of fooling around with cultic and occultic doctrines and belief systems.

Use Your Resources

Apologetics is on the cutting edge of Christianity. The reason why there is so much hostility toward it is because it is the search and use of pure truth. Once the searching Christian gets a taste of the effect and power of its potential, nothing else will ever compare or satisfy his thirst for such knowledge. If this Christian continues his pursuit and realizes that he can begin to answer his own questions and expand his search into all avenues of religion, science, philosophy, or even politics, he will become unstoppable as an avid studier of the Word of God and a relentless soul winner. He will also realize that the field of study is inexhaustible.

When I first began this study, there were only about five men or so leading the way. Researchers used to say that apologetics was the best-kept secret in Christianity. Hardly anyone had ever heard of it. Now there are hundreds, perhaps thousands of websites and ministries involved in cult evangelism. There is no reason why Christians from all walks of life cannot take advantage of this virtual explosion of knowledge, especially when it is so easily accessible on the web. We are no longer confined to mountains of books and hours of time making copies of material. Just about anyone can find access to a computer and print out tons of material on just about any conceivable subject.

Satan has been very carefully leading the world up to a time when people's minds, spirits, and hearts are fully prepared to accept and worship the beast and follow him gleefully into Armageddon (the last great war), terrible eternal darkness, and the lake of fire. This is why being a student of world events and or the big picture is of such importance to the individual Christian. Apologetic researchers are seeking to equip people with all the knowledge and materials they can to wage war against this landslide of sin and wrong philosophies that fight to control the minds and hearts of every person on this earth. Christian researchers are not interested in impressing people with their great storehouse of knowledge (as some might assume). They are seeking every way they can to get knowledge out to other people, where it can be used to the greater advantage. (And if you have a bad memory like me, you can use paper and tapes like I do.)

Without Jesus Christ in his heart, that person is already deceived. That person may possess really good morals as far as the outside world is concerned. But the ultimate spiritual darkness remains an empty void that needs desperately to be filled with the love and hope of God himself through the person and atonement of Jesus Christ, the Savior of the world. But most of the world rejects the love of God and the Bible as absolute truth. They will not accept Jesus Christ as Savior into their hearts for whatever reason they have conjured up in their own minds.

The root of political correctness is already there for the unbelieving mind. Satan simply takes that root and expands it until in the end it will take over almost everything but for a very short time. In the meantime, all of the evil that permeates the world right now will only continue to mount and get worse. What is the answer? The nonbeliever needs to become a believer. And the Christian must arm himself with love and knowledge and try to educate himself and others in order to show—are you ready?—that God is the ultimate answer through the cross and he loves us enough to suffer and die for us.

In other words, God loves us. You and me, I mean. The answer is truly the simplicity of the gospel of Christ. John 3:16–17 says, "For God so loved the world that he gave his only begotten son; that whosoever believes in him will not perish but have everlasting life. For God did not send his son into the world to condemn the world; but that the world through him might be saved." The Bible says that because of the fall of man from grace in the garden of Eden, mankind is born into sin. He needs to be born again of the spirit. Jesus said in John 3:3, "Verily verily [this is important, this is important] unless a man be born-again he cannot see the kingdom of God."

Apologetics a powerful tool we can use to reach the lost for the kingdom of God today. I think it would be beneficial to Christians to at least get their feet wet and give it a try before we discount it with our own internal prejudices. The unbelieving world accuses Christians of being against the progress of scientific knowledge and philosophy and being out of step with our increasingly complex world. I am not saying that we, as Christians should take on the world's values. However, I am saying we can prove them wrong by studying things that will help them better understand God and his Word. Second Timothy 2:15 says, "Study to show thyself approved unto God, a workman that needeth not to be ashamed, rightly dividing the word of truth." First Thessalonians 5:21 says, "Prove all things; hold fast that which is good." Second Corinthians 2:11 says, "Lest Satan should get an advantage of us: for we are not ignorant of his devises."

The temptation here is to become angry or sarcastic trying to prove an unbeliever or a cultist wrong while trying to persuade them. We must try to remember the purpose of using this powerful tool, and that is to convince folks that Jesus is indeed the Savior of the world, not to prove that we are right and very knowledgeable. Most folks who practice apologetics have made this mistake at one time or another and have had to spend time to correct the error. (Okay, I'm guilty.) But this is a very common error among us, and eventually God will show the better way as we open ourselves to him. That is the most important part of using this material. Remembering to stay in prayer and asking God to help us understand it and use it in the right way is of the utmost importance. It is also important to help other Christians to understand the study if they are not aware of it so they too can use it to help others and win souls.

A good scientist sees a mystery and knows he must do his work and research to find an answer. It may take a long time and a lot of patience, but in the end, his work is rewarded. Why not begin today to use apologetics to help others come to know the Lord? You might be surprised at the results.

Chapter 4

WHAT ABOUT THE CULTS?

Just a few years ago, the word *cult* was virtually unknown to the average person. Today however, cults have put themselves in the forefront of the news headlines and become a heavy concern in the boiling arena of world problems. But just exactly what is a cult anyway?

Even from a purely Christian point of view, it is difficult to define a cult. The late Walter Martin said that a cult is a bunch of people gathered around somebody's interpretation of the Bible. The reason we say the Bible is because many of these cults focus on it and try to reinterpret it or to rewrite it. The Bible positively condemns such practices. Second Peter 2:1 says, "But there were false prophets also among the people even as there shall be false teachers among you, who privily shall bring in damnable heresies, even denying the Lord that bought them, and bring upon themselves swift destruction."

Saving Grace

Cult leaders quite often claim to be God or Christ and claim they have a new insight into spiritual things that pertain to God and that they are talking directly to the Father. This idea would be virtually unknown to modern-day Christians since Jesus already said he has gone up to sit on the right hand of God and has sent the comforter or the Holy Spirit to be our guide here on earth. Talking directly to the Father is a privilege that was left to the Old Testament prophets. Old Testament prophets usually carried a message of doom and gloom for Israel because they were involved in too much sin. If the Jews were going to take heed of these warnings, then all of Israel would have to follow all the instructions of the prophet exclusively.

Today we are given a new kind of freedom under the New Testament known as the dispensation of grace. Through the death and resurrection of Jesus, we are freely given permission to come to God in prayer ourselves and not through a priest or a prophet. We are also given the freedom of grace in that all we have to do is ask for forgiveness in prayer and God immediately gives that forgiveness without needing the permission of any man or any other being in heaven or earth. Grace simply means that through the cross God gives us love, compassion, understanding, and especially forgiveness even though we don't deserve it. Ephesians 2:8–9 says, "For by grace are ye saved through faith; and that not of yourselves: it is the gift of God: Not of works, lest any man should boast." Mark 3:28 says, "Verily I say unto you, all sins shall be forgiven unto the sons of men, and blasphemies wherewith soever they shall blaspheme."

This of course means that if a person is willing to believe in the Lord Jesus Christ and is willing to ask him into his or her life and ask for forgiveness, then all sins, no matter how serious, will be forgiven him or her. There is no need to ask another person, or meditate, or climb a mountain to ask a guru. The work is already done on the cross. Jesus said, "It is finished."

It doesn't get any easier than that. There is no need for further complications. The Bible has made a way for all to come to God, and it is not the exclusive privilege of one person or even a group. The redemptive or forgiving power is already there just for the asking.

But as we can see, false leaders want to make things more complicated and muck things up. Why do they want to do that? I believe it is first because they want to feel important to a large number of people. They crave the love and adoration of these folks and can never get enough. Second, there is control. If they can control folks and make them believe they (the leaders) are God, they can of course acquire anything from them, including money or sex. Intellectuals of our day have accused the Bible of being oppressive, but when we get down to a real study of grace, we can see a much different picture. That picture shows us that the Word of God offers freedom to come to him ourselves and even to worship him without any interference from an outside source.

Authority over the Bible

False prophets also take the position that they have writings that are above the power and authority of the Bible. For some odd reason, people get the idea that the Bible is incomplete or doesn't provide enough insight for mankind, and something must be added to help it along. It may be true that the Bible doesn't tell *everything* there is to know about our world or our universe. It stays on the subject of personal salvation and gives us rules and guidelines for mostly our spiritual and moral life. It says God created the universe but doesn't explain *how* he created it. We are then left with a vast dimension of mysteries and questions that seem beyond our ability to grasp. Although science and philosophy have come up with some answers to how the universe works, we are still in a fog, with many difficult questions, both physically and spiritually. If God knows everything, then why wouldn't he simply reveal all to us now? Why play this game?

I think the answer to that is very simple. The Bible has revealed to us what is required to attain forgiveness and enter the kingdom of God, no questions asked. It tells us of the tremendous effort it has taken to bring us to a point in history where we could understand his plan of salvation, even though it is very simple. Nevertheless, the Bible is still a very thick book. It takes a long time to read it and forever to understand all that went on, especially in the Old Testament. If God were to reveal everything about heaven and earth, it would certainly take more than one book; it would take more books than the whole solar system or even the galaxy could contain. God focused on what was needed, and that was the salvation of the human race or redemption from sin, a way of reconciling the human condition, which is initially separation from God and his love and forgiveness.

Even with this one book and one Christian faith, there are still hundreds of denominations and folks contending over all sorts of things within its context. Just think if God had written many more books and tried to explain further what salvation, heaven, and hell are all about, the mysteries of the universe etc. I think such information would only cause more confusion and delay to mankind rather than help it. It's best to keep things simple if possible, and I think God has done this as much as it can be done. We may live in a very complex world, but personal salvation through Christ is the most important thing of all. After all, what is more important than determining where you or I will spend eternity? Nothing that I can think of.

Also, what if God did suddenly reveal everything there is to know about everything? What would be left for us to do? We could build any machine, cure any disease, conquer any problem, and virtually be gods ourselves. The way things are, we are left to dig and search for the answer to problems and mysteries ourselves. We must not only search heaven and earth for the answers to why nature acts the way it does but search for a better way to get along and love one another rather than try and destroy one another.

Jesus emphasized love more than any other factor in the Bible. Sometimes this seems an impossible task with all the evil that goes on around us. Our first thought is to react to our circumstances rather than to find a way to love. This is a monumental task for the Christian and for humanity in general. But it is something we can strive for as well as the quest for knowledge. In other words, God has left us with immense challenges. Isn't that what life is all about?

To further complicate matters, false leaders will constantly make the statement that they are always getting new truth from God. This goes back to what I said before about the Old Testament prophets. We don't always need advice from someone who claims to have a new vision or revelation from God. We already have his plan of salvation in our hands. Cults quite often require that a person hand over his will to some supposed higher authority rather than that person making decisions for him or herself, hopefully with prayer. To me, this is very dangerous by itself. A person claiming to be a prophet, messenger of God, or God himself could give a command that is supposedly from God to do something terrible. If people have already handed their will over to this all-knowing person, they are left with a horrendous choice. Either they can defy the cult leader and face the supposed spiritual consequences or they can go along with the evil he has commanded and face the possible earthly consequences. What a terrible choice!

Along with this giving up the will comes the worship of a person or an organization more than God himself. A documentary video entitled *Gods of the New Age* showed followers worshipping Bhagwan Shree Ragneesh, a former cult leader in Oregon a few years ago. This segment of the video was eerie because it showed his followers gathered around him in orange outfits and jumping up and down and waving their arms in total adoration of this Eastern guru. Many Eastern religious leaders actually claim that they are greater than God. People who follow such mystical leaders agree with this idea. The only viable reason people would go along with this idea is because they have handed their reason and free will over to a flawed human being and now believe everything that person tells them.

Another disturbing factor in the Oregon case is that many of these devoted followers were very educated people. There were doctors, lawyers, engineers, and so on, totally committed to the new cause. Many of them handed over not only their minds and wills but also all of their material wealth. Why? Because of what I mentioned in the first chapter. People get tired of the material world and start desperately searching for something to fulfill them spiritually. Highly intelligent and creative people can end up on the most vulnerable list of potential followers a lot of times because they have already achieved what our society considers the greatest success. They have attained the big college degrees and the material wealth but feel that great vacuum inside that only the real God of the Bible can fill up. Satan knows all of this and tries hard to divert people from knowing that simple truth.

Redefining God

Another thing false organizations do is redefine the Jesus of the Bible and make up another Jesus. This can be very subtle. The Bible pronounces many times over that Jesus is God. In Exodus 3, Moses was inspired when he saw a burning bush on the side of a mountain and climbed up to see why the bush was not consumed by the fire. At this time, the Jews were being held captive as slaves for the Egyptians. God explained to Moses that he had chosen him to go back to Egypt and lead his people to freedom.

Up until this point, God had not really revealed any official name for himself to Israel or anyone else. Moses asked God what he should tell them when they asked who had sent him. God said to him in verse 14, "I Am that I Am. Tell them I Am has sent you."

Of course, we are going to ask, "Why did he say that?" I asked that question myself. There are two or three reasons. First, there are a lot of people who say God isn't or he doesn't exist. God here is saying, "I Am. I exist. I am here." He is also saying something about his nature in that he says, "I Am, I was, and I always will be." Greek scholars say that the actual word used there for "I Am" comes from the word *Elohim*, which means "he who is to be." This is a very powerful verse because it has to be one of the earliest signs of the coming of Christ.

Now let's cross reference this and compare this verse to John 8:58 of the New Testament. The scene is set at the Mount of Olives, and Jesus was arguing with the scribes and Pharisees (the religious leaders of his day). He had pronounced to them many times his authority and the fact that the Father himself sent him, yet they seemed to feel the need to challenge his position and ask him who he thought he was. In verse 58 Jesus said, "Verily, verily I say unto you, before Abraham was I Am." He was saying he was the same guy who talked to Moses on the mountain; there is no difference.

The Old Testament says that if a person claims to be a seer or a prophet but turns out to be false, he should be stoned to death. The Jews considered this the ultimate blasphemy and picked up stones to cast at him. They were hostile toward Jesus and knew exactly what he was saying, and that is he made himself to be God. It would be impossible to get around the fact that he made the claim to be God just from this one verse, but there are many others (John 1:1–14, 10:30, Heb. 1:8, Phil. 2:6, Rev. 1:1, 8, Isaiah 48:12, Rev. 22:13).

False prophets who claim to be Jesus are easily seen as false because the Bible says that Jesus already died on the cross for our sins and ascended to heaven (Acts 1:10–11). No man standing on earth can say that he is the Jesus of the Bible because the next time people on earth will see Jesus is the day he returns in power and great glory (Matt. 24:27).

I have belabored this point because cult leaders and false prophets almost always try to get around it somehow. They try to lessen the authority of Christ to lift themselves or their organization up over it. When you look at their situation, they are really left with no choice but to grapple with it because they are trying to elevate themselves to that level to gain and keep control of a person. It's obvious that from the context of the Bible, Jesus has made this very heavy claim to be God. At this point, there is no getting around the fact that he is either a raving lunatic, frothing at the mouth like some of the cult leaders we have heard from, such as Jim Jones or David Koresh, or he is who he said he was. There is no in between.

We are left with a quandary here. Either we can believe that the Jesus of the Bible is God and give him our love and adoration, or we can blow him off and say the Bible is completely wrong. The reason I say this is because in our day and age, people have often said Jesus could have been a very smart man or some kind of gifted person who knew how to do ESP or some kind of moral mystical character rather than someone we should worship. But according to the Bible, he claims to be much more than that. We are left with a decision to either believe what he says or throw it out completely if we are honest with ourselves.

But many of the cults have set out to completely obscure this fact that he is actually God and have attempted to give him a different definition. When people do this, they are moving sharply away from the traditional understanding of Jesus' personal work and nature. We are then left with a different Jesus who does not fit with the biblical teachings of who he is. The New Testament writers were aware of this slippery sleight of the hand act from Satan. Galatians 1:8 says, "But though we, or an angel from heaven, preach any other gospel unto you than that, which we have preached unto you, let him be accursed."

I have heard it said that the way we can recognize a false prophet is to get to know the original so well that we can easily recognize the counterfeit. This statement is very true, and we should get to know the Word of God very well. But it is also important that we do our research and read and check out what preachers and teachers are writing and saying. This requires that we read *their* material in order to figure out what they are trying to tell us. It is important too that we check out some of the researchers and apologists. I have come across some very bogus apologetics in my own studies. It's good to use the research of others, but it's also good to do some of our own checking into the original material of the writers and preachers. *If we are going to challenge* a preacher, teacher, or writer about his integrity, we had better make very sure we are right in our assessments. This will save us a lot of embarrassment if we are wrong.

Understanding the Trinity

Cults usually reject most traditional Christian beliefs and make up their own. They are also hostile toward anyone who disagrees with them, including other cults. One of those traditional beliefs is the Trinity.

In the early days of Christianity, there was much confusion about what was to be believed about the three-fold manifestation of God. He has appeared to us in three different ways, yet the Bible proclaims very definitely that there is only one God. Eventually a definite understanding of the *Trinity,* emerged which helps us understand how God reveals himself to us.

We have the manifestation of the Father, which most of us don't have any problem with (Rom. 1:7, 1 Cor. 1:3, 2 Cor. 1:2, John 8:41). I have already explained that Jesus is God. The Holy Spirit also claims to be God in that Hebrews 9:14 says the spirit is eternal. So we have three persons in the trinity and one God. How could this be?

Water exists in three states—solid, liquid, and gas—yet it is still water in all three states. There are many chapters in a book yet it is still one book. These are common illustrations of how the trinity can exist in a three-fold manifestation. But there is something more we need to take into consideration here, and that is the understanding of other dimensions. God lives in another dimension. How can we understand this? I believe we can only understand this up to a point.

Hugh Ross, a Christian astronomer, gave this object lesson on understanding other dimensions. We live in our own dimension, which is the physical dimension. It has height, breadth, width, and time. We don't know what another dimension might consist of, but we can look at it this way. Imagine that we cut out two paper dolls and laid them on a flat table. We will call them Mr. and Mrs. Flat. These two figures are in another dimension because they would be unable to comprehend the rest of the room full of televisions, chairs, walls, and so on because all of these objects have height and breath. The only way Mrs. Flat could see all of Mr. Flat is to walk all the way around him, and then she could only understand his outline since she couldn't see all the way around him at the same time. The same if true for us because we can't fully understand God and all he is simply because he lives in another dimension.

Time flows in one continuous line for us and is unstoppable. We get old whether we like it or not (and most of us don't like it). But for God there is no time in his dimension. He and his kingdom are eternal. From his dimension, he can see everything at the same time. He can also see what is going to happen and all of the past at the same time because he is not held down by the strict laws that govern our dimension. If you were to put your hand down as close to Mr. and Mrs. Flat as you could it without touching them, they would never know you were there. That is how God can be so close to us yet we can't see or comprehend his presence. When God breaks into our dimension and changes something, we see this as a miracle. For God this change would be no big deal and perfectly normal.

The reason I brought all of this up about other dimensions is because there has been so much confusion about the Trinity and understandably so. I have already talked about the fact that there are mysteries in the Bible, some of which can be searched out and understood from much study and research. But there are things about God we will not understand until we die and go to be with him on the other side. That is because there is no way we can understand or comprehend another dimension while we are in this one. We are given physical bodies that are adapted to our physical universe and all that exists here. Our soul is held captive inside our space suit of the physical body until we die and it is released to be with God. He has *revealed* himself in three persons to our dimension but is still one God, which we will fully understand on the other side.

One of the best illustrations of what God is was demonstrated the popular movie *Raiders of the Lost Ark*. At the end of the movie, God comes out of the box or ark, and his spirit floats around the room in a magnificent display of his awesomeness and power. This is what God would be to us—a spirit. John 4:24 says, "God is a Spirit: and they that worship him must worship him in spirit and in truth." Some of the cults, such as the Mormons or the Church of Jesus Christ of Latter Day Saints, have said that God is a man of flesh and bones very much like you and me.[1] But in the

---

[1] Patrick Matrisciana and Ed Decker, *The God Makers*. (Jacksonville Beach, FL: Jeremiah Films, 1990).

light of both Scripture and logic, this is a rather serious error and tries to change the definition of who and what God is. The Mormon belief system is therefore labeled a cult from a Christian point of view.

Look Cool

False religions also try to make a favorable impression in the public eye. Their missionaries wear nice clothes and are taught how to present their cultic views to unsuspecting folks by trying to look like squeaky-clean Christians themselves. These missionaries are taught what to say and do not reveal everything their system believes. This can be very deceptive because even members of the very cult itself don't know everything they believe. Many cults do social work and build hospitals or do outreach programs to the poor. But we must remember the basic ingredient of becoming a real Christian: salvation through *grace* and simply believing in the person of Jesus Christ. *Not by works lest any man should boast,* as Paul said.

In general, we basically have two kinds of cults: the isolationist cult, which requires that members move in with other members in some sort of housing and stay there, and the type that just requires much church attendance in a church type of setting. This is not a rule carved in stone, however. Heaven's Gate, the UFO cult that recently committed mass suicide, roamed the country and lived in various places until they received a large contribution from a wealthy businessman and were able to acquire housing. Cults generally make up their own thing, so it's hard to make strict rules for recognizing them in some instances. But if we understand the Bible's definition of who God is, we don't have to worry too much about making up rules about cults.

False Date Setting

Many times false teachers are also overly concerned about the book of Revelation and the last days. This is to put fear in the hearts of their followers to keep control of their will. Sometimes false teachers will make up a date for the end of the world. But Jesus said in Matthew 24:36 says, "But of that day and hour knoweth no man, no, not the angels of heaven but my father only." Any earthly person who sets a date for the beginning of the tribulation is just wrong in his assessment and understanding of Scripture. The world has gone through many upheavals and wars through time. Many things have to happen before the actual return of Jesus.

If we read and understand Bible prophecy, we will begin to understand that we can assess the world through the Bible and create a balance in our belief system. This is not to say that we should just stick our heads in the sand and say it will *never* happen. I have heard many folks say the book of Revelation is full of symbolism and is impossible to understand. They further pronounce that God will never bring such a harsh judgment on the world. But since the Bible was accurate in predicting the coming of Jesus to earth in the flesh, it follows logically that the book of Revelation will open just as assuredly. We are not in control of these events; God is. To pronounce that we know when it will happen or that it will not happen is in major error. These things must be left up to God and to God only.

I have not gone into the specifics of the various cults here. It is extremely important that my readers take the time to look through and get some of the books from my reading list. These can be used for reference when a question pops up about false teachers and cults in various forms. Another thing you can do is find a computer with Internet access and simply type the word *apologetics* into the search engine. You will find a whole new world inside these websites.

But be careful about the Internet. Everyone knows that all of the information there is not always true. I will also leave the address of some websites I know to be very legitimate. But remember what I have been talking about in this book about the last days and heavy deception. It is possible some of these ministries practicing apologetics will get something wrong just because they are imperfect humans. But as the world moves toward the end, even legitimate ministries of all kinds could fall away into the darkness of deception. In some instances, this has already happened. So please be careful, and check things out for yourself.

Chapter 5

THE CHURCH IN CRISIS

I have mentioned that there are movements within the church that are teaching that we as Christians should never get upset or angry about anything. I find this concept to be one that comes from the world viewing the church and not really from the church viewing itself. It is one that the church has taken in over the years, but it is not one that the Bible really teaches.

Let's say you found yourself in an argument with someone over a serious problem. As the argument goes along, you begin to realize that the person you are disputing with is not really upset about it at all. The first things that come to your mind are that this person must not really care about the subject very much. They don't take you very seriously and brush it off without much consideration. As a result, the confrontation accomplishes very little, and the problem more than likely continues to be a problem.

I heard a popular preacher say in a sermon that a person that never gets mad about anything is generally worthless. This concept is a major factor pushing us to the last days and the judgment of God and can be labeled *apathy*. Much of the Christian world seems to think that the problem of false teachings from within and without the church is not very important, or they think we are not supposed to be upset about anything and therefore turn an uncaring face to the wall. I have found this to be the case with quite a few Christian leaders and lay people today.

It seems increasingly popular to turn away from problems, such as false teachers and the cults, especially when it comes from within. We have heard the old cliché, "I live in a pretty good neighborhood," and it applies very well to today's Christian church. I will grant you that keeping a straight doctrine is not all there is to being a Christian. In a way, this is the easiest thing to do once a person understands the basics. But when a movement, preacher, teacher, or organization threatens the very core of our belief system, this problem should not be ignored. Just exactly what am I getting at? Well, to explain that, let me tell you something about myself.

I was very atheistic or agnostic before I accepted Christ into my heart and was born again in early May of 1978. I guess I became rather atheistic around the age of thirteen because I thought science and modern philosophy had all the answers. Nobody seemed to have answers for questions I had about the nature of the universe, creation, or philosophy.

I became very discontented at the age of sixteen, and after a very horrible argument with my parents, I ran away from home with a friend of mine. We bought some Greyhound bus tickets and went to Louisville, Kentucky, where we tried to join the army. Well, the recruiters soon discovered we were just lying about our identity and our age and called our parents on the phone, trying to figure out the best way to come and get us.

My brother came to Louisville, and it was a dark and moody drive back home. After we got back, I was awakened by a sheriff with a flashlight in my face at about 3:00 a.m. I spent an emotional twenty-four ours in the county jail and was finally taken to court, where I saw my parents for the first time in two weeks. I was judged an unruly child and placed on probation for the next six months or so, but I decided to join the army since I was almost seventeen. I talked my parents into signing the release papers.

While in the army, I met Mike, an American Indian, and we became fast friends and had much in common. Mike was heavy into New Age thinking (only we didn't call it that back then). I think the thing that interested me the most was soul travel or astral projection. I dabbled in the occult with Mike, and we talked about our interests in science fiction, philosophy, and the occult. I was searching desperately for some meaning, some purpose for our existence here on earth.

After I got out of the army, I remembered some folks in the barracks talking about some books about an Indian philosopher who mixed thoughts with sorcery to gain access to powerful knowledge and other worlds. I didn't get a job right away, so I had time to sit around and think about life at time.

I had been hitting the bars pretty hard on the weekends, a habit I learned rather well in the army. One of these bar excursions was particularly memorable. I was coming back home with a friend, and we were firing down the highway like a jet fighter. Suddenly I felt the very real presence of Jesus in the backseat of the car. His presence was so strong that there was no denying it. He spoke to my heart that everything was going to be all right. Just then my friend lost control of the car, and it went across the opposite side of the road, hit a telephone pole and a sign, and flipped over upside-down. We were shook up and went to the hospital with only a few cuts and bruises. Well, as you might have guessed, my atheistic ways were changed just a little.

Just a few months later, my American Indian friend (Mike) came to visit me from Oklahoma. He told me that he had become a Christian. I was stunned! We used to sit around together and watch television preachers just to make fun of them. The knowledge that Mike had become a Christian had a major impact on me.

We went to McDonald's to have coffee, and I told Mike about my experience in the car accident and about the feelings I had there about Jesus. As we were talking, Mike tried to tell me about God and how I needed to get saved. I was rejecting it on the outside, but I was thinking on the inside about the car incident.

"Bunk!" I said to him. "I don't need that stuff about God."

But while Mike was getting refills, I suddenly felt the presence of Jesus again, as I did in the car. He spoke to my heart and said, "You know, Jeff, you have turned over every rock of inquiry and asked every question imaginable. Why don't you just let me in?"

And I did let him in. Even before Mike got back with our refills, I was born again. My life will never again be the same.

During this time of my life, I was what you might say a little wild in a way. I didn't want to just get a job and settle down somewhere. I wanted to roam around and see the world. I thought working was stupid in that it held down a person's potential. Mike was about the same way. I also believed a person didn't have to work and that God would just provide all of your needs by faith. This proved true over the years to a degree, but I don't think I would ever want to try some of the stuff we tried in those years again.

To make a rather long story short, Mike and I traveled and drifted over various parts of the country for about the next eight years. We learned a lot about God and met some cool people and some not-so-cool people in that time. But at one point in time we decided to visit the PTL Club (Praise the Lord) in Charlotte, North Carolina. It was at the time the largest television ministry in the world, hosted and owned by Jim and Tammy Bakker. At the time, I was fascinated by Christian television.

We arrived at the PTL Club in late fall, and the warmth of summer hadn't quite arrived yet. Jim Bakker was just planning to build Heritage USA, a very large area he had purchased on the outskirts of Charlotte. We eventually migrated to a woods, where we stayed just outside Heritage. We made our way onto the grounds, attended many of their church meetings, and watched the television shows that were broadcast from the Heritage church there.

But Mike and I were living in the most primitive way imaginable. We were dirty and smelly most of the time and had no vehicle for transportation. Heritage was a rather big place, consisting of estimated at least one hundred acres of grassy lands. It consisted of huge campgrounds, a small lake, and a place where folks rented cabins. It would take some time to even drive around the grounds, but we walked everywhere we went. There was a tour tram folks used to get around on the campgrounds and to attend church services, and we rode on it extensively, but for the most part we marched.

The first thing we noticed about their behavior was the security guards. They watched our every move like we were escaped convicts. I remember one time in particular when we were on our way out of the grounds and became exhausted. We had some sleeping bags and stopped that evening and laid down behind a small hill and made camp there that night rather than trying to make it to our place in the woods.

The next morning we were on our way down the road out when a small security car stopped us and began asking questions as to whether we had slept on the grounds. We finally admitted we had. They informed us that we were not to sleep on the grounds unless we had a tent and paid for a camping spot and stayed there. Run-ins with the security guards there became an almost routine event during our visit there, which lasted about nine months. We were asked if we were Christians on many occasions, and I might say we were drilled on the subject. I'm sure many of the PTL staff and security weren't convinced we were saved because of our physical condition at the time.

The Word of Faith Movement

As we went along, we began to understand the beginnings of a new doctrine floating around in Christianity and big time at PTL called affectionately the "prosperity" doctrine. It is known now by several names: "health and wealth," "the word of faith movement," "name it and claim it," "the signs and wonders movement." It claims that by following certain "faith formulas," a Christian can become perpetually healthy and wealthy and never have to face the hardships of poverty again. We, of course, were much interested in this doctrine at first and wanted to know how it worked so we could use it to overcome our own condition.

As we attended many of their meetings, a pattern emerged in their belief systems. We noticed from personal experience that Christianity in this area was deeply affected by this doctrine. Many of the people who visited PTL were rather wealthy and were therefore mostly unreceptive to folks in a lower or even middle-class economic status. We learned to hide and evade those we knew to be on the unsympathetic side. The ministry was certainly nothing like I imagined it to be from watching it on television, and I became very disillusioned after a short time of being there and doing the escape and evasion thing.

I can now of course understand some of the hostility toward us because we were unemployed at the time and had to depend on part-time labor and the mercy and charity of others. But I am glad now that I saw the prosperity doctrine from that particular point of view. They taught that a Christian should follow the faith formulas to be a prosperous and victorious believer marching in tune with God's plan of the day. This made our condition much worse because it made people less compassionate toward poor folks.

Eventually, as you might have guessed, Mike and I parted ways. I went home, got a job, and settled into a normal life. But the prosperity doctrine still bothered me in many ways. I could see the arrogance of it in many ways in the churches I visited over the years since, but for a long time I just couldn't put my finger on exactly what was wrong.

In the years that followed, I became very familiar with the study of apologetics and learned how to recognize false belief systems rather effectively. Then a friend of mine told me that the Christian Research Institute was talking on the radio about the prosperity doctrine. I learned that this was headed up by Hank Hanegraaff, the new administrator of this ministry. He and his staff had spent hundreds of hours studying this movement and had found out some very powerful problems inside it.

Dan McConnell, who did graduate work at Oral Roberts University, traced the history of the movement back to a man by the name of E. W. Kenyon in his well-researched book *A Different Gospel.* Kenyon was deeply influenced by the mind science or metaphysical cults in the early 1900s.

The thoughts of Kenyon were copied by Kenneth Hagin and later much more widely popularized by Kenneth Copeland. Now let's take a look at exactly what this movement believes.

They say that God is a being very much like you and me and that he stands about six foot two to six foot three, weighs a couple of hundred pounds, and has a hand span of about nine inches. That God created this world through visualization (a very old occult practice). They say God created earth as an exact duplicate of the planet where God lives.[2] They also say that Adam and Eve are not just reflections of God's being but that they are exact duplicates of God. Now Adam and Eve are not even subordinate to God. In other words, they are free agents now. They do not have to answer to God's authority in any way. Benny Hinn has said that Adam was a super being who could fly through space and even to the moon. But because Adam and Eve ate the fruit, they took on the nature of Satan.

> Adam had become the first person to be born again; he was "born" with the nature of God and "born again" with the nature of Satan. God was then banished from the earth desperately searching for a way back in. Through a deal made with Abraham promising him tremendous wealth God regained authority back into earth. This story continues on to say that Jesus descended into hell and was tortured by the devil and his demons. Satan realized that he had made a legal error though. He realized that Jesus had never sinned so he had to release him. Jesus then emerged back on earth and born again.[3]

---

[2]   The whole fable of what this movement believes can be found in Hank Hanegraaff, *Christianity in Crisis*. (Nashville, TN: Thomas Nelson, 2012), 19–23.

[3]   Ibid., 23.

Another major problem with this doctrine is the belief in a thing called "positive confession." By constantly repeating the right words and the right belief in these words, you can have what you say by speaking things into existence. One of the most often quoted Scriptures taken out of context in support of this wrong theory is Romans 4:17, which says, "As it is written, I have made thee a father of many nations,) before him whom he believed, even God, who quickeneth the dead, and calleth those things which be not as though they were." Of course, since Christians are given this extraordinary power, they can call things into existence from nothing, just like God—that is, if they do positive confession correctly. (This has always been confusing to me. I could never figure out how this formula is supposed to work from talking to Christians who believe in *positive confession*.)

The next major problem is our definition of faith. Faith is viewed in this context as a force like electricity or fire. It is supposed to have substance in the physical realm like any other force. Through faith in your own faith, you can speak things into existence through positive confession (confused yet?). God even uses faith here, and so he is pronounced as a faith being (not space being?). This is why this doctrine is then termed by researchers as the word of faith movement.

The next phase is a belief in perpetual health and perpetual wealth. Christians are not supposed to ever be sick or without money. If they do suffer from sickness or poverty, then they are either still in the learning stage or are not doing the positive confession thing right yet. Years ago I wrote to Jerry Seville and asked him how the formula was supposed to work since I was myself very poor at the time. He wrote back and said that you just have to stay at bat until you hit.

The Bible talks a great deal about greed and materialism. Television preachers say that to receive God's blessings, you must first plant a seed with their ministry or in other words send money to them. There have been not a few news documentaries on the overpowering wealth of some of these television preachers. Although I don't believe it is a sin to be rich as a Christian (depending on where your heart is), we need to remember that Jesus was born into poverty and died in poverty. In Matthew 16:26, he said, "For what is a man profited, if he shall gain the whole world, and lose his own soul, or what shall a man give in exchange for his soul?" Matthew 19:24 says, "It is easier for a camel to go through the eye of a needle, than for a rich man to enter into the kingdom of God." Revelation 3:17 says, "Because thou sayest, I am rich, and increased with goods, and have need of nothing; knowest not that thou art wretched, and miserable, and poor, and blind, and naked."

All through this doctrine, we have the promotion of humans to gods and the demotion of God to a lesser power. We find the promotion of Satan and the lowering of Christ to a lesser throne. I have already talked extensively about how cult and occult belief systems practice this idea at length. It is the oldest lie of Satan from the third chapter of Genesis when he told Eve that if they would eat of the forbidden fruit, they would be like gods.

This is one of the biggest reasons I believe that the word of faith movement is a major move on the chessboard of Bible prophecy toward the last days. It seems that much of the human race have a desire to be like God or to be gods themselves and to have complete control of their environment. In a way, this is a very appealing and tempting idea. I think at times we would all like to have God's power to change things in the world around us to where we would like them to be. But we need to remember the concept of free moral agency here. God in his infinite wisdom has opted to give us free moral agency. He allowed this thing to happen as a result of the fall of Adam and Eve in the garden of Eden. If we were given the power of God, we would also be given this problem of deciding how much we should interfere in the affairs of men and cross the line into their freedom of choice. In other words, with power comes a heavy responsibility. It is the same as what happens to a person when he or she is promoted to a manager position.

The Bible predicts this great falling away from the truth as the last days come upon us. If Christianity carries the truth about Christ but is caught up in the belief that we humans are gods, then a vast portion of the church will already be in agreement with the antichrist before even climbs up on his dark throne. What opposition will he then face if Christianity is in agreement with him?

Apathy

One of the worst problems I have run into in the area is apathy. I have talked to some church leaders and pastors, and the response is downright as scary as the doctrine itself. They don't seem to care. They just say, "Oh well. Christians on TV and in churches these days are just not theologians." (Theology means the study of God.) The problem with this response is that people have died as a result in believing in the perpetual health doctrine. The word of faith teachers have taught for years that you should deny the symptoms of ill health (pain, etc.) and stand on faith that you will be healed or that you are already healed. Larry and Lucky Parker wrote a book called *We Let Our Son Die*. They kept back insulin from their son, and he eventually died.[4]

In his book *Disappointment With God*, Philip Yancey points out a word of faith church that must maintain a high security profile (have lots of security guards around) to protect themselves from angry people who felt deceived when they followed the unhappy road of prosperity formulas and someone in their family died as a result.[5] How then can church leaders, especially pastors, continue to ignore this problem? How can they continue to stay silent on this subject when people's lives are being wrecked or have even faced death? How can the Christian layman ignore this problem even when friends and family are caught up in it?

Christian Martyrs

Let me take this a step further. Jesus said that in the last days, folks would kill Christians thinking they are doing God a service. How could that happen? Very simple: the ones who are killing the true Christians are following the wrong god. Through all these ages, Satan has been preparing the unbelieving world for

---

[4]   Ibid., 61–62.

[5]   Phillip Yancey, *Disappointment with God*. (Grand Rapids, MI: Zondervan, 1997), PAGE NUMBER(S).

the introduction of the antichrist. Furthermore, 2 Thessalonians 2:3–4 says:

> Let no man deceive you by any means: for that day shall not come, except there come a falling away first, and that man of sin be revealed, the son of perdition; Who opposeth and exalteth himself above all that is called God, or that is worshipped: so that he as God sitteth in the temple of God, shewing himself that he is God.

Let's take a look at 2 Timothy 4:2–5:

> Preach the word; be instant in season, out of season; reprove, rebuke, exhort with all long-suffering and doctrine. For the time will come when they will not endure sound doctrine; But after their own lusts shall they heap to themselves teachers, having itching ears; and they shall turn away their ears from the truth, and shall be turned unto fables. But watch thou in all things, endure afflictions, do the work of an evangelist, make full proof of our ministry.

Could this doctrine be one of the major factors contributing to the downfall or the falling away as Scriptures foretell? I personally think it could be. Many Christians who have been involved in this movement have given up hope and left the church because they found out the faith formulas didn't work. The great majority of the church is ignoring the problem as it creeps around in many different forms and infections. There are some involved in this movement who go to church every Sunday and every Bible meeting. They are getting a heavy dose of the wrong Jesus and are not really born again. This is a major problem. How do we tell them that everything they have been hearing for all these years is messed up? Wouldn't that discourage them? Well, I know we have to tell them anyway, but you see my point. This doctrine causes all kinds of major problems from within the church and from without.

I have gone into great detail about the word of faith movement because I believe it is a powerful contributing factor leading up to the opening of the book of Revelation. What leads up to the judgment of God in the last days is what is most important to us today and in this book. For the Christian who wants to stay informed in today's world, Hank Hanegraaff's books and audio tapes *Christianity in Crisis* and *Counterfeit Revival* are a must.

I have already stated why I think this subject is of monumental importance—because it may very well have much to do with the fact that the Bible predicts a great falling away just before the beginning of the great tribulation. The well-informed Christian can use these books and tapes to educate the folks around them about the problems connected with it.

This doctrine is extremely dangerous in many ways. Besides the fact that it causes many folks to stop taking medicine and die, it also redefines who Jesus is like all the other cults. But it is very subtle too. It's almost impossible to recognize from just a surface glance. Much of what we know about the universe is like that. Many folks, even scientists, believed that the sun and stars revolved around the earth for a very long time until more sophisticated methods were discovered that proved this idea very wrong. It has taken a lot of painstaking hours of very competent researchers to uncover this movement for what it really is. It is a very good fake, and it is being spread throughout the world on the Trinity Broadcasting Network every day. These are excesses coming mostly from the charismatic world, and they are becoming more excessive as time marches on.

Christianity has faced very powerful false movements in the past and survived them. But today we must face the vast power of electronic media. It is a growing problem the church must face head on in the next few years if we are to overcome it in any fashion. But I believe it will be one of the major factors in the weakening and falling away of many believers in the last days and will very much contribute to the rise of the antichrist in the end. With Christians floundering in false doctrines and the immoral behavior of the world rising, we are looking at a monumental catastrophe in the near future unless a vast majority of Christians rise to the occasion and take up the banner for Jesus to fight against it very soon.

The Latter Rain

From the word of faith movement came another spin off of a sort of neo-Pentecostal or super-Pentecostal movement known by some researchers as "the latter rain." Some other names would be "counterfeit revival," and some call it the Vineyard movement. The Vineyard is a church started by John Wimber, who was a man who desired to see miracles because the Bible talks about miracles. The only problem with this idea is that we cannot manufacture our own miracles. We must wait on God to manifest them.

The latter rain really goes all the way back to the 1940s, which was a sort of post-revival time for America. People began to yearn for the old days when the spirit was so strong and powerful and won many souls.

During this post-revival time, people like A. A. Allen and Oral Roberts showed up, and divine healing became the in thing of the day. As this movement began to grow, it began to use radio and television. Along with television and radio's magic lure came a rather large bag of beautifully wrapped books and tapes to help people understand how to get their healing and keep it.

But in recent years, the latter rain movement has moved radically away from even so-called radical Pentecostal circles and has become its own creature, so to speak. Out of the Vineyard movement came the new latter rain, and people in Toronto Airport in Canada began speaking in tongues, howling like dogs, laughing like hyenas, crawling on the ground, and snorting like pigs. Very little attention is given to the written Word of God in this movement because that would interfere with the fun they are having outside of what the Bible has to say about such behavior and belief systems.

Along with the latter rain comes a lot of prophesying. People who claim to be prophets are proclaiming all sorts of interesting things. First and foremost important to the movement is a strange idea that there is going to be a bloody civil war between orthodox Christianity and the latter rain folks, which I guess will determine the truth about who is right.[6]

What exactly does this mean that there will be a bloody civil war between orthodox and latter rain people? That's a very good question. I don't think anyone really knows at this point, but it doesn't sound good. I have read testimonies of folks who have had family members who got involved in this movement who ended up in divorce or worse. There are folks who have been shunned by other members because they refused to believe in the prophecies and messages given by the latter-rain prophets. This movement has unfortunately spread throughout the world and the United States and is growing. Many non-charismatic and non-Pentecostal churches are completely unaware of this movement here in America but need desperately to know about it because it has a way of taking hold.

The popular movement known as Promise Keepers was started by Bill McCartney and James Ryle, who were and are very much part of the latter rain movement. Promise Keepers has been reported as being rather ecumenical in that it allows other belief systems in to become a part of its belief system. This report is not hard to believe because Promise Keepers preaches and teaches unity all the time. But many researchers believe that this unity is at the cost of sound biblical doctrine. (Recommended readings and references on this topic are *Promise Keepers, Another Trojan Horse* by Phil Arms *Beware the New Prophets* by Bill Randles.)

---

[6]   Hank Hanegraaff, *Counterfeit Revival*. (Nashville, TN: Thomas Nelson, 2001).

Another organization I am very cautious about is the Willow Creek Association or the seeker-sensitive church in Illinois. This church, started by Bill Hybels, tries to find ways to get people into the church by way of modern technology (which is not all bad), but I think this church is dangerously on the edge of changing the message of the gospel by leaving out the preaching of the conviction of sin. A person cannot come to salvation or a heart conversion without knowing first that we have sinned and come short of the glory of God according to Romans 3:23. Many of these churches have become so modern that it tunes out the very much-needed voices of the past that come straight from the Bible. The bottom line is that we need to get back to the basics of sin, salvation, and repentance, not move further away from them for the connivance of others' personal comfort. As Christians we are to conform the world to Christ, not change the church for the world.

The rule of thumb today is to keep a very close watch on these powerful and growing para-church organizations that make all of these claims to fortune, fame, and divine healing. Once these organizations and clubs get inside the church, they are very hard to get out. The average congregation gets hooked on them and will violently oppose any move to disengage from them. Any pastor who might be brave enough to stand against them now would face severe persecution and opposition from his congregation. If a person doesn't believe there is a spiritual power behind these types of organizations, I give you a challenge. Try opposing it some time. You'll find out the truth very quickly.

Liberalism

As if the word of faith movement were not enough, we have an even bigger problem with liberal doctrine. This is another problem from within the church, and it can be hard to recognize at a surface glance. When I first got saved, I found it hard to believe that there could be people within the church who deny belief in the divinity of Christ, the trinity, the resurrection, the virgin birth of Jesus, and in the true nature of miracles. What is left?

What is left is an outer covering or shell. Second Timothy 3:1–5 says:

> This know also, that in the last days perilous times hall come. For men shall be lovers of their own selves, covetous, boasters, proud, blasphemers, disobedient to parents, unthankful, unholy, without natural affection, truce breakers, false accusers, incontinent, tierce, despisers of those that are good, Traitors, heady, high-minded, lovers of pleasures more than lovers of God. *Having a form of godliness, but denying the power thereof: from such turn away.*

Matthew 7:15 says, "Beware of false prophets, which come to you in sheep's clothing, but inwardly they are ravening wolves."

With a little study, we can recognize the cult attacks from without the church. Their doctrine and way of life become obvious after some passage of time. But the liberal doctrine from within is much more deadly. Christian leaders and pastors are telling us that the power of the Bible is no longer legitimate. Many denominations and facets of Christianity are infected with this belief system, and it is growing. Leaders of this powerful movement have gained ground and influenced other Christians on a massive scale. We have much controversy over the acceptance of homosexuality and abortion and the acceptance of other belief systems into Christianity. These issues should not even be a question to the Christian church. Yet it is being debated between denominations and Christian leaders as if we could make a precedent over the authority of the Bible.

Those who teach liberal doctrine say that we can take whatever parts of the Bible we want to believe and throw the rest out. This is to say that we as fallible human beings can decide by way of our own wisdom what is inspired by God and what isn't. This is another instance where the sinful nature of the human condition has taken over and tried to skirt the power and authority of the Bible. If we are not going to believe the Bible is true on all counts, we might as well throw it out the window and find another religion. Skeptics and agnostics do the same thing. They take parts of the Bible, put them together, and make up their own god. But redefining God apart from his Word is a grave error and will eventually bring about God's final judgment on the world.

Beware of these false liberal teachings that deny the power and authority of God's Word. These types of churches also do all kinds of social work and outreaches but are against the main purpose of the church: reaching lost souls for Jesus. Evangelism is the most important arm of the body of believers on earth, and it must not be ignored if we are to please God with our faith and good works.

If the liberal doctrine is true, then the death of Jesus was of no effect. Then the sufferings and death of all the prophets and martyrs through the ages means nothing. The great hymns such as "Amazing Grace" are of no great consequence and should not be sung. If liberalism is true, then all of the testimonies of those who were taken out of terrible sin were just wishful thinking and didn't really happen. The book of Revelation is no longer applicable, and there will be no judgment of the world, as some have predicted.

During the reformation led by Martin Luther, many folks actually died in the midst of the battle to bring the gospel forward to the average person rather than keeping it in the hands of higher church authorities. According to this doctrine, then all of their deaths were in vain for a mystical dream of one called Jesus.

All of these problems stem from a general breakdown in morality and faith. If we want to be true Christians, then we must understand some of what is going on in the world. The trouble with that idea is that most Christians are not interested in checking out the big picture. What is leading to the tribulation or God's final judgment is what is most important to us today. But questions will arise from time to time about what will happen in the end. It is important too that we be able to answer questions about Bible prophecy. This is the subject of my last few chapters. But first we need to talk about the great falling away or the great apostasy.

The Great Apostasy

We are coming into an era even in our own time in which the church as we see it now will eventually crumble and fall away. The buildings will all look just fine, but what is going on inside will be the deciding factor and the true temperature gauge telling us what is really happening.

I have had a lot of people ask the question, "Falling away from what?" Well, falling away from their first love—the Lord Jesus Christ—and the true teachings of the Bible. The first three chapters of Revelation tell us of the many problems and hazards of the condition of the church in the very last days. One of the biggest problems with the church today is a rise toward materialism, which is to begin to step away from God. Revelation 3:17–18 says:

> Because thou sayest, I am rich, and increased with goods, and have need of nothing; and knowest not that thou art wretched, and poor, and blind, and naked: I counsel thee to buy of me gold tried in the fire, that thou mayest be rich; and white raiment, that thou mayest be clothed, and that the shame of thy nakedness do not appear; and anoint thine eyes with eyesalve, that thou mayest see.

It is obvious that Jesus is telling the church that materialistic riches of this world are unimportant compared to the riches of the spirit and what can be gained by following the true teachings of Jesus into the next life. But the church of our day cannot see this teaching very clearly, it seems. It seems to the outsider that Christians are more concerned about what car they are going to buy than what they believe and do for Christ, who died on the cross for them.

We live in an age of convenience. If something gets in the way of our pleasure and comfort zone, we generally try to get rid of it so we can go back to normal. We cannot even imagine what it would be like to be as committed to the gospel of Christ as were the disciples or the apostles of the early church. There are loving, devoted Christians throughout the world who would and do give up their very lives for the gospel, but I believe they are the exception and not the rule on a massive scale.

I have devoted much time and many words in this book to show the reader the importance of knowing who the real Jesus is and why we should follow him. And I have devoted much work to show how to recognize the true and the false. I have also shown how the world and the church are falling into a great deception as time goes by, such as political correctness and the word of faith movement. Why? Because Satan has taken the time to bring the world to the point that they will accept the presence of the antichrist with few or no reservations. In other words, by the time the antichrist is revealed to the world, the church will be so deceived it will not know who he really is and even help bring him to spiritual and political power! This is a horrible tragedy beyond words. The very institution that should be the foundation and salvation of the world actually betrays the one who bought them at tremendous price and takes sides with Satan against him and without really knowing it. How awful! That's putting it mildly.

The great apostasy can be seen in several different arenas and quadrants of the world. We have a great portion of the church flopping on the beach of false doctrines and another great portion drowning in liberalism. Then we have the conservative evangelical church, which is supposed to be holding out and standing up with and for the truth seemingly, without mercy and without love.

Maybe my readers will think this is mostly subjective and prejudice, but I feel the need to express a great concern here. If a person were to just get up one morning and decide to walk into one of the conservative churches, what is wrong is not always immediately evident or even noticeable. Let's say that our person doing the church searching is at least fairly well informed and knows the basics. He knows it is important to check into what this particular church believes. Well, when he looks in the church manual, he finds that all seems well. The basic essentials are there. They believe that Jesus is God and in salvation by grace and so on.

But after being at this church for a few months, he has taken note of several major problems. First of all, he finds that the church is constantly begging for money for this project and that building. The preacher is constantly hammering away that giving is of the utmost importance and that tithing one-tenth of your income a major priority in the Christian life. He finds this rather disturbing because this seems to take precedence over spiritual things of greater importance.

He has also most unfortunately noticed that many folks in the church seem preoccupied with the cares of this life and seem to have little interest in studying or reading anything that might help them understand the Bible better. Theology and apologetics are virtually unknown to the average Christian mind, and political correctness is the order of the day. Many, though they don't really say it out loud, *don't really feel the need to press the issue when it comes to doctrine.* When asked about the subject, most church people express the need to say, "We are not supposed to judge anybody no matter how corrupt that person's doctrine is. Love is the order of the day, and we have to accept people whether they agree with us or not." This, of course, is not at all what the Bible teaches, but it is a popular notion that most people embrace today without question. They say we should be building bridges, not barriers.

Finally, he reluctantly takes some of these concerns to the pastor. What is the pastor's reaction? The problem is there is little or no reaction at all except, "Well, I'm sorry you feel that way, brother. The church is not perfect, you know. Come back and see me some time."

Now our friend becomes rather flustered and frustrated with the lack of spirituality in his newfound church. But while he is contemplating these things, he begins to find out other things that are even more disturbing. He finds that people who call themselves Christians are drinking heavily, living together outside of marriage, and proposing that the Bible is not really that accurate, even in Sunday school and other places. And they have a general lack of interest in what the Bible really says. He finds that even though the church manual states everything correctly, on paper at least, most of the people attending don't understand the basic essentials and have no idea how to defend it or explain it. Ironically he finds many of them actually arguing against some of the essentials.

This is very discouraging and very confusing to our church searcher. So he goes out from this church and begins to look around in more conservative evangelical churches, only to find basically the same problems everywhere. Is it possible that the conservative church has failed too and fallen away from the truth just as much as the other more obvious ones in error? Yes, I'm afraid they have and are falling rapidly away, as you might have suspected. In the writer's opinion, most of the church of today is reeling in darkness and is basically in a deep sleep or coma and is totally unaware of the approaching disaster that is about to follow the great apostasy.

Another sign Jesus gave about the end and the downfall of the church comes from Matthew 24:12: "And because iniquity shall abound the love of many shall wax cold." Lightly translated he is saying that because lawlessness shall be plentiful (lots of it), the love of many shall become cold (dried up and ready to blow away).

I have stated in a few places where I believe that the church (conservative evangelical) is waning and starting to give way to the last-days apostasy like a great dam leaking and seething from so many cracks that it eventually gives way and crumbles, leaving great destruction in its wake. It is an institution that has stood for two thousand years through great hardships and great persecutions, but the major portion of the religious Christian world will not survive the last-days judgment and tribulation. Why?

It has been the author's perhaps again subjective observation that the Christian church is greatly lacking in the agape love the Bible describes. The Word of God tells us that we are to love one another as God has loved us. I suppose there might have been a time when Christians were more caring and loving than they are now. I said that when I first got saved, I spent time on the streets with my American Indian friend. We very much noticed that hardly anyone was willing to take the time to help us or even straighten us out. There were times when Christians would find out about some of our false doctrines and would chastise us or try to refute us. But we often wondered, if they really cared about us, why no one took us aside for a while and explained from their storehouse of knowledge why we were wrong in doctrine and practice. I think we would have been hard to convince, but I don't think the task would have been impossible.

Since I have been off the streets, I have been to many churches and observed many things about the lack of love in them. I have often wondered why pastors constantly ask for money for big, beautiful buildings instead of using it for building a homeless shelter or a new program for helping people with their bills or handing out food. There are obviously going to be people within the church who are hurting financially and in other ways who could benefit much more from loving gifts of money and kindness than from a new building. This flaw is most obvious to the unsaved world and is quite often pointed out by them if you talk to them about the gospel in any way. *If the unbelieving world can recognize this flaw, why can't the inner circles of the church?*

As even Christians experience this lack of love, they become discouraged in their walk and their own self-esteem is lowered, as well as their expectations of themselves. As time goes on the church becomes little more than a social club with a hint here and there of a group of folks who were once empowered by love, and the Holy Spirit, and selflessness rather than selfishness and self-centeredness.

There is an overflow of problems people are experiencing in the church today, such as emotional disorders. Folks who experience this problem are advised to see Christian counselors and psychiatrists. But in my avid opinion, most of these disorders could be solved if Christians simply took the time and made the selfless sacrifice to take some of these broken spirits in and love them until their problem disappear. There is a hunger inside each one of us to love and be loved by others. If a person in the church is alone or experiencing some difficulty, it is up to others to help him or her with love, prayer, and self-sacrifice rather than simply sending them to a counselor.

If I may express a personal observation, I have noticed another aspect of the church that is even more disturbing. I have at times talked to Christians in the traditional church about things that were going on in my personal life. I talked quite a bit about some of the satanic oppression that permeated my life and how I needed prayer and advice. Many times when I expressed this problem, I was met with empty stares or just skepticism.

I didn't understand this reaction from church people for a long time. I thought there must be something wrong with me. Then it occurred to me that this was not the case. I had always maintained through my Christian walk that there was something dreadfully wrong with the contemporary church. But now I know they are simply not discerning. They don't understand the awesome power of God, and neither do they understand or comprehend the powers of darkness. *I hate to say it, but I think the real truth of the matter is that a majority of the present-day evangelical church members are not born again.* How did I come to such a drastic conclusion?

Most evangelical preachers and teachers today teach that a person can simply come forward in a church, come to the altar, pray a simple prayer of salvation, and be born again at that moment. I think this may be a very dangerous assumption. Over the years, I have heard many folks in the church express the fact that they have heavy doubts about their salvation. Pastors constantly try to console them and tell them that it's natural to have such doubts from time to time and just to rely on the Word and not on their feelings.

What is very dangerous about this type of thinking is that it is partially true and partially not true. Although we cannot rely on our feelings and emotions about everything when it comes to the true Word of God, it is also true that when you become a new creature in Christ: "Therefore if any man be in Christ he is a new creature, old things are passed away behold all things are become new" (2 Cor. 5:17). Something tremendous happens inside.

When a person really and truly gets saved, he is changed in an instant from the road he was once on to a completely new road—the road of salvation. The thought of the heart changes, that person's worldview changes, and light comes in where darkness once ruled. When I think of myself, I know that when Jesus came into my heart, there was a total spiritual awakening within me. I knew that just a moment before I was hostile to God but I was now a friend and an accepted disciple of his love and grace. There could be no doubt that something had happened inside me to change my heart and mind completely. Not that I would never sin again, but I had the assurance that I was now a Christian and would enter to the gates of heaven through his mercy and grace, for now I knew the difference between the light and darkness that existed inside of me. Lights came on and bells rang inside my soul. I was truly redeemed even though I had little knowledge of the Word of God. I still knew I was changed and would never again be the same.

I have noticed with great concern that a great many Christians of our day do not seem to share in this tremendous experience of being really born again; many Christians I talk to seem to have a rather swampy and vague notion of what has happened to them. They seem to communicate that nothing of that sort happened to them. They went up to the altar of the church and prayed a simple prayer asking Jesus to come into their hearts, and nothing really happened at the time. Then later on something seemed to be different, and they took that to mean that they were really born again. I think there is something very dangerous about this type of reasoning within the church.

I don't think that any person, whether they are attending church at the time or just wandering around in the unbelieving world somewhere, just wakes up one morning and says, "Hmmmm ... I think I'll just get saved today." A person begins a sometimes rather long journey to salvation by beginning to search for truth. The truth he or she finds along the way may or may not have anything to do with preaching or the church or Christianity in general. If a person is really and sincerely searching for truth, God will begin to move obstacles and mountains out of the way and begin to shine his glorious truth to them through any means that will reach that person. He will use circumstances and challenges. He will use books and assorted wisdoms from any corner of the earth that will begin to open that person's mind and heart to the saving grace of Christ.

Every person's barriers and questions are different, and God knows this and finds what appeases the heart and mind of the sincere and brokenhearted searching person. After many realizations and perhaps even hazards, that person reaches a point where he or she no longer sees the world's concepts as valid. He or she begins to see the real truth of God—that it is the eternal things that count and not the temporary worldly wisdoms and materialistic consumption of things that makes the great difference. It is through the revelation of God to this person that he or she begins to have many very powerful realizations that begin to expand the mind and fill the heart that eventually leads to salvation and the acceptance of Christ into one's heart and soul.

Now it is possible that at the right moment that this person could be in a church and hear the call to the altar and find themselves kneeling and praying there and receive the born-again experience. That is very possible. Very often, though, many true believers accept Christ outside of church through this realization process and then find their way to church later.

There is another kind of path many take, and it is a much harder one. Paul said in Romans 5:20, "Moreover the law entered, that the offense might abound. But where sin abounded, grace did much more abound." Of course we all know that sin does abound (is plentiful) these days. We live in a day when sin is taken lightly, and everyone has gone their own direction. It seems to find more of it than anything else. A person who gets caught up in heavy sin, such as drugs, alcohol, sexual perversion, crime, deceit, etc., begins to feel the terrible consequences of his or her acts. Newton's law says that to every action there is an equal and opposite reaction. Galatians 6:7 says, "Be not deceived; God is not mocked: for whatsoever a man soweth, that shall he also reap." In other words, what goes around comes around.

Eventually the evil this person is doing catches up with him, and he ends up in a hospital suffering from gunshot wounds or in a prison and suffering from the consequences of his acts. As a result, he begins to realize there is no way out. This will begin to work on his mind and heart, and he will begin to be visited by God in several different ways. God will begin to reveal his Word to him through people or reading or experience until he realizes he has fallen into a trap that only God can get him out of.

Romans 3:23 says, "For all have sinned and come short of the glory of God." He fully realizes that he has sinned and come very short of God's required holiness and righteousness, and his heart becomes heavy and sorrowful for what he has done. He knows that without a doubt, his sin is more than he can bear. At that moment, he asks God to come into his heart and forgive him of his many terrible sins. This is when he finds the true born-again experience and becomes that new creature in Christ Paul talked about in 2 Corinthians.

In this way, we come to realize that many times it is the bad people who make it to heaven, and the people who think that they are okay with God because they have supposedly been good all their lives end up in hell. Why? Because it is the saving grace of God alone that can get us to heaven and nothing of ourselves ever. Isaiah 64:6 says, "But we are all as an unclean thing, and all our righteousness are as filthy rags: and we all do fade as a leaf; and our iniquities, like the wind, have taken us away." Ephesians 2:8-9 says, "For by grace ye are saved through faith; and that not of yourselves: it is the gift of God: Not of works, lest any man should boast."

Everyone who is truly born again knows we cannot come to the realization of God's grace on our own brainpower. When a person searches for truth, God sees that person's sincere heart and carefully leads that person to a point of true repentance and a reception of his presence into his heart so he is truly saved into the kingdom of God. That person will then stand before the judgment seat of Christ on the day of judgment as a saved person and has his name written in the book of life. This wonderful state of affairs happens to him rather than him having to stand before the great white throne judgment, where God will explain to him why he is going to spend the rest of eternity in the lake of fire (Rev. 21:8).

Having said all this about the born-again experience, I have to conclude that many folks in the church think a simple, glib trip to the front altar will somehow provide them with hell insurance. Then believe they can go about their lives without a single change in their hearts, minds, souls, or lives and still make it to heaven. I hate to even think about the rude awakening that may be waiting for them on the day they die. I always hope against hope that this will not be the case in many Christian lives. But I'm afraid the condition of the present-day church may very well present this awful, horrendous truth to many on that terrible day. Hebrews 10:31 says, "It is a fearful thing to fall into the hands of the living God."

Another problem with the present-day church is its hierarchy and involvement in politics within its own structure. Pastors and other leadership positions are paid professional people. If a problem arises, such as a false doctrine within the denomination, few if any of these paid-position people are willing to put their jobs on the line to begin to solve the problem. Our call as Christians at times is to lay our proverbial heads on the chopping block and take the risk of losing our platforms, jobs, or popularity. This, of course, is not an easy thing to do, but it is the only right thing to do in some instances.

We must not forget folks in our past who were willing to lay down their very lives if necessary to preserve the gospel or to stand against evil. One of the biggest problems with this within the traditional church is the fact that many of these pastors and Christian leaders are career people. They are never to jeopardize their positions or their jobs just for the sake of the truth of the gospel or for the welfare of others. American Christianity on a large scale has become too convenient and easy and a form of religion that denies the power of God in many ways, as is already stated in 2 Timothy 3:1–5.

I have already discussed in some detail the problems with Christian television and how they are promoting false doctrine throughout the world on a massive scale. One of the biggest things I noticed about the televangelists is that they have become sacred cows or icons to much of Christianity. But there are also many sacred cows within the evangelical church too. These are the folks we can call big shots, I guess. They are like the megastars of Christianity. They are singers and preachers that are hoisted up in the lights, and many have become as rich and famous as the movie stars of the world.

This hoisting of people into the limelight does not seem to agree with Scripture in several ways. The Bible calls us as Christians to be humble and to esteem others as even higher up than us. We are not called to find out who is the greatest within the kingdom of God but to shine our light in a way that does not let our left hand know what our right hand is doing. Many of the themes being preached from the pulpit of these sacred cows has to do with supposed spiritual success, which also, of course, includes popularity and monetary gain.

Jesus said in Matthew 19:24, "It is easier for a camel to go through the eye of a needle than for a rich man to enter the kingdom of God." First Timothy 6:10 says, "For the love of money is the root of all evil." It seems to me that Christianity, while following the road to riches, has decided to follow the exact opposite road that the Bible calls us to follow. How can Christianity call the world to conform to Christ when Christianity has already conformed to the world's standards? Slick programs and popular speakers and singers are the order of the day. These popular singers and speakers come up on the platform claiming that what we need in the body of Christ is unity while competing with each other for popularity and book and record sales tooth and nail, just like any worldly business. There seems to be little difference between the two.

I think the only cure for all of this madness is a total reform and return to the simplicity of the gospel. Christians who are serious about their walk with God may need to leave the traditional church someday and find a rational faith in home churches and in small gatherings with true believers who do not find their faith in the Christian entertainment media or the heavy-handed denominational, institutional church. It's time for us all as Christians to face the truth. Christianity is in desperate need of repair and reform in many ways. If this does not begin to happen soon, I believe we will begin to see the beginning of the end or the last days as described throughout the Bible. It is the church that God uses and the people within to win souls and keep the world from spiraling down into complete moral decay. But when the church reaches that point of moral decay itself, our world is in desperate trouble. And in desperate trouble it is today, whether we like to face it or not.

I cannot sit down and logically show you the love temperature gauge and be able to tell you how much love has diminished since the first primitive church. But just reading the book of Acts in an informal way will immediately tell us that the church of today reflects very little of the fire and love that came from the beginning. History tells us that Christians of long ago were willing to lay down their very lives for one another as Jesus laid down his life for us. The lack of love and mercy in the church of today is its greatest problem and is contributing to the burning fuse toward the end of time and the antichrist more than any other factor. Why? Because if the church was willing to love as it used to, many more folks would be saved, and many more would hang around to improve things around them, especially the lives of others.

In other words, the love of many has already waxed cold. The unbelieving world will not come or comes very seldom to the church for help or salvation because they see no difference between the merciless church and the merciless world. They are both about equal. Can this problem be remedied? Well, Martin

Luther brought about the great reformation during impossible times. And many other men who walked with God brought about a change where no change seemed forthcoming.

So yes, I think the true believers within the church will someday somehow bring about reformation. As time goes on though, in my opinion, we may eventually have to leave the present church completely and meet in homes or basements as the last days approach. This is only my opinion, however. But I lay it out there for whatever it's worth. I have also come to realize that there are indeed thousands of Christians spread throughout the world who are true believers, but they are fragmented, and many of them are facing the problems of being Christians alone. Our greatest challenge as true believers is to find a way to come together. I'm open to suggestions. May God bring us all together in the true prosperity of love and in the true power of the Holy Spirit. Amen.

Chapter 6

THE APPROACHING JUDGMENT

As the big hand of the clock moves closer to midnight and the blade of the guillotine drops down, Jesus' description of the condition of the world becomes more serious, and the trials and tribulations of poor old mother earth become worse. The hour of tribulation he describes as *the beginnings of sorrows* in Matthew 24:8 paints a picture of the darkest times this world has ever seen.

In verse 9 of the same chapter, he says that whoever follows the teachings of Christ will be taken and afflicted. (Afflicted means having trouble, pain, or sorrow put on you by others or by circumstances.) Verse 9 says, "Then shall they deliver you up to be afflicted, and shall kill you: and you shall be hated of all nations for my name's sake."

Jesus is giving us a graphic view of the condition this world will be in during the time of the last days. He is warning us that the curtain that holds back the forces of evil will be rolled back, and believers in Christ who will not compromise their position of faith will be taken to prison, brutally abused, and even killed.

Those who have always held the position that Christians are just a bunch of religious fanatics and should be eliminated finally will be given a free hand to show their disdain in violence and corruption. The forces of the antichrist are beginning to show themselves more openly, and the gates of hell have opened wide to flood this world with its final assault on the gospel of Christ, for Satan knows his time is short, and he has only a few moments before the Lord of glory puts a complete stop to him and his demonic activities.

In this time, we are beginning to see a terrible cloud of darkness and oppression fall. Evil men will become more and more open in their attempts to stamp out the light of righteousness or any hint of true morality according to God's Word. This verse seems to indicate a tremendous change and worldview as to how we treat our fellow man, and a wave of madness takes hold to lay hands on anyone who disagrees with the new system of thought. Believers' faith will be put to the test in the worst way.

In verse 10, he says, "And then shall many be offended, and shall betray one another, and shall hate one another." Offended by what? What could everyone be so offended about enough to betray close friends and relatives? Well, it has become quite obvious by now that the world situation has changed on our prophetic map. People have almost totally given in to their earthly sensuous desires. They do not want their indulgences in sin and wickedness to be interrupted or challenged in any way. By now they have almost achieved that goal. Powers that are in charge of governments have changed to such a degree that the tables have turned. It is now legal to be a criminal and illegal to hold up the banner that stands for true justice, righteousness, and good. Men and women who were once held up as connoisseurs of making the world a better place to live and workers of good are now taken to prison, tried and convicted, and killed for their once well thought of accomplishments.

In Luke 21 Jesus said Christians shall be taken by force, taken into synagogues, and brought before kings and rulers. Skipping down to verse 16, he says, "You shall be betrayed by both parents and brethren, kinfolk and friends, and some of you shall they cause to be put to death."

By now the trap Jesus spoke of that would come upon the world unawares has been sprung. The snare has been pulled tight, and it looks as though evil has finally triumphed. Satan has tightened his grip, and it looks as though the Holy Spirit is choking and Christians are gasping for their last breath. The last remnants of the gospel have been all but snuffed out and the fire of its message of glorious salvation and eternal life put out.

But take a look at verse 13: "And it shall turn to you for a testimony." Now we're getting somewhere. Jesus is saying in the next two verses that Christians *will* be given their say after all. The Holy Spirit is not choking. In his attempt to stop the message of salvation, Satan has fallen into his own trap.

Luke 21:15 says, "For I will give you a mouth and wisdom, which all your adversaries shall not be able to gainsay nor resist." God has given Christians their greatest hour in history here. The Spirit of the Lord is shining bright in the midst of the thickest darkness. Now that things have changed and persecution has intensified to the point of making martyrs of believers in Christ, we can clearly see the implications. The testimony of a man about to be put to death for his unmovable convictions has to have the heaviest impact of all. No one would dispute the fact that there has to more to his faith than mere religious fervor. He must be real enough in his rock-hard stand for Christ to actually die for him.

The victory for Christians in the future wrath of God upon this world is right here in front of them here in this Scripture. If we are willing to lay down our very lives for our beliefs, then surely this kind of testifying will move the unmovable mountain, shake the unshakable atheist, and change the hearts of perhaps masses of the spiritually dead. What a glorious opportunity to show how we really feel about our salvation.

Moving on to verse Matthew 24:11, it says, "And many false prophets shall rise, and shall deceive many." Here again we have the second warning against false prophets. The deception has grown deeper in this stage, however. Satan is throwing all he has at this world now, and I'm sure the magnetism and drawing power he possesses have increased greatly. People will see the popular movement toward anything that is spiritually flashy. He says here that they will deceive many. It will become much more difficult to resist this movement toward the false prophets for two reasons. First, it will be difficult because of peer pressure to be part of the crowd. No one wants to feel left out of the party. You could be looked down upon by your friends and family as odd for not joining in. Second, it could cost your very life eventually, whether you are a Christian or not. Just the very fact that you have not succumbed to the pressure will cause you to stand out like snow in August.

Verse 12 says, "And because iniquity shall abound, the love of many shall wax cold." (I know I'm repeating this verse but in a different light.) We can see this happening even now as the world moves closer to the end. The word *iniquity* simply means sin, corruption, and lack of self-restraint. If we were to reword this verse, it might read like this: because sin shall run unchecked, the love of many shall burn out and grow cold. Today's society is full of corruption, and things happen every day that are beyond our control. Every night in the news we see the craziness of senseless wars and violence, and who hasn't had the feeling of throwing up one's hands and saying, "What's the use? What can I do as one little person with no talents?"

But it is exactly here that we have utterly missed the point. We are not here to change the world from outside in. We are here to change it from inside out. Let me illustrate what I mean. When you watch a talk show on television and they are talking about some problem or another that is plaguing a community, you always hear the same solutions. The women's rights movement is trying to pass a law through congress. Minorities are trying to pass a law to force businesses to hire them anyway. To slow down crime, they suggest taking self-defense classes and having longer and tougher sentences for criminals. They are trying to change the world by trying to put pressure on people through laws, regulations, and force. But that is not the message of the gospel. I, as a Christian, am not trying to change this world to paradise. I am not trying to bring heaven to earth. I am trying to change the hearts around me to Jesus Christ. Then that person will no longer have the desire to commit crimes and to act unlawfully and so on. Jesus said the kingdom of heaven is within us. We really can't change a man by badgering him with the fear of consequences. The only way to change a person is through the love and mercy of Christ, which will eventually affect his or her heart.

Here we have another victory over the seeming rampage of evil that is coming upon the world. Even though the love of many is waxing cold around us, we as individuals can still stand for Christ and love our fellow man regardless of how unpopular our convictions are.

Let's look at verse 13: "But he that shall endure to the end, the same shall be saved." Verse 14 is really a stickler: "And this gospel of the kingdom shall be preached in all the world for a witness unto all nations; and then shall the end come." I have thought, as many people, that this bit of prophecy would happen before all the things described in the book of Revelation would take place. As we know, much of the world has already heard of Christ and been converted. However, as time has passed, I have begun to see a different light in this particular passage.

When the time comes that Christians are arrested for their unmovable convictions and brought before rulers and magistrates, Jesus stated that no one will be able to argue them down or resist their rock-hard testimony. He said that he himself would give them a mouth of wisdom and not to worry about what to say beforehand. Here we can see that certainly the Holy Spirit is in full operation and he cannot be shut up with the threat of death or violence.

This kind of testimony would certainly have a tremendous impact on its listeners. Probably hundreds, perhaps thousands of people would be changed because of these powerful encounters. The power of the Holy Spirit would change the average Christian from lukewarmness to being a mighty prophet of God! The word of such a powerful testimony happening over and over around the world would spread like wildfire! Man may be able to kill these brave martyrs' fleshly, earthly bodies, but their testimony of what God has done for them will put a thorn in Satan's side that will linger undaunted until the end! The gospel could be preached to the entire world by the average nobody Christian of today!

Verse 17 of Luke says, "And ye shall be hated of all men for my name's sake." There has always been persecution of the church. The Romans threw Christians to the lions. Paul had his head cut off for his efforts. All of the prophets of the Old Testament were persecuted, and most were murdered. Even today we hear of Christians being jailed and even murdered in various countries for their undaunted beliefs. The thing that sets the last days apart is that the entire world will be aware of the truth of the gospel and will set out to wipe it and its people from the face of the earth. History books that include anything about God may be cast into fires. Houses of once-respected citizens may be broken into. There may be kangaroo courts in which trials could be held to get rid of these people who once stood as a standard against sin. Now we are getting a clear picture of what it will probably be like in the last days before Christ returns. It will be most unpopular and costly to stand for Christ in these dark days. But it will also be a time when I am most sure that God's people will empowered of his Spirit, for the Lord will not forsake his people. Hebrews 13:5 says, "I will never leave thee, nor forsake thee."

Another aspect of the world's condition is the failing economy. As pressures mount and more institutions buckle and go under because people are unemployed and desperate, the world will spiral toward the cashless system of the antichrist. As of now, government programs are less than adequate to meet their needs. Minorities, the poor, and the old are the hardest hit by these cracks in the system. With all this comes the feeling that our present system has failed us. Worldwide inflation continues to climb at different intervals, and even those who hold jobs are hard pressed to continue their standard of living. An atmosphere of tension is created, and many feel unfairly treated. This could easily push the United States and other countries back to a situation much like the sixties. Riots could occur that could turn the world upside-down. We are looking at a strong possibility of economic collapse starting in either America or Europe. This collapse could cause a major shift in governments and usher in a time that is just right for the new world order to take over. Economic pressures and failures can do one thing. They cause people to look for a way out—to look for something or someone to pull them out. That something is the subject of my next chapter. See ya there.

Chapter 7

KING KONG, GORGO, AND THE BLOB

Neither shall he regard the God of his fathers,
nor the desire of women, nor regard any god: for
he shall magnify himself above all. (Dan. 11:37)

There is mention of a mysterious figure all through the Bible. This individual is to rise up and deceive the whole world into believing he is the man who can save the world from all its problems. Who is this man? What is his goal?

He goes by several familiar names: the antichrist, the son of perdition, the beast, son of Satan, king of Babylon perhaps, the little horn of Daniel's vision. I don't know how many times he is mentioned in the Bible, but I do know he is mentioned enough times that he cannot be overlooked or ignored if we are not to be caught unawares. God started warning us over two thousand years ago about the antichrist. He warned us of this monumental event as far back as Ezekiel and Daniel. These prophets knew nothing of our present technology and world condition, yet they give us a startling picture of what we should be ready to encounter when we see this mysterious figure rise to power on the world scene.

(Interpretation of Scripture in Bible prophecy can be hairy at times. You may sometimes strongly disagree with some of my concepts. Some things about Bible prophecy will probably not be fully understood until they actually happen, so we can certainly disagree in good conscience about some of its aspects. I do believe, however, that we can derive enough from Scripture to receive an ample warning and to prepare our hearts and minds for the worst of times this world has ever seen. I pray that all who read these words will take heed and be found worthy to escape the wrath of Almighty God during this most dreadful hour.)

The antichrist has been studied and speculated about for a number of years. I have heard him labeled different people, different presidents, the pope, secretaries of state, and various dictators, such as Hitler and so on, ranging from the sublime to the ridiculous. What sober conclusions can we come to from a serious study of the subject? Well, first of all, information about the antichrist cannot lead to eternal life. Only those things that tell us about Jesus Christ can lead any human being to the road of salvation. Certainly it seems that there has been enough written about the antichrist to keep a person entertained and speculating for years to come. My major purpose here is to *warn the reader rather than entertain him.*

Perhaps only twenty years ago an event such as one man taking over the world was unthinkable and even laughable. But since world events have left the earth in the mess it's in, hardly anyone is laughing any more. Among perhaps not-so-recent events but highly significant is the reestablishment of Israel. That tiny nation that is so hard to find on my big world atlas is to play a major role in the coming years of the man of the hour, the beast.

First of all, the antichrist, according to Bible's description, is a man who will rise to power in the end times just before the return of the true Messiah. He will rise to power when certain conditions have been made right for his takeover. I have already discussed many of those conditions in my beginning chapters in a way because he is not really unlike many of those who have preceded him. The false Christs, messiahs, and prophets all carry with them the same qualities that he will have, only on a smaller scale. Hitler and most other dictators had many of the same qualities also.

As I have said, our world is moving in that direction in many ways. The fear and insecurity that sin, violence, crime, and dishonesty have created have paved the way for his appearance. The recent movement toward an interest in the paranormal, ghosts, UFOs, and occult activity has been preparing the masses for the intrigue of his spirit and made it easier for him to convince others that his seemingly magical powers are real and unchallengeable.

But his power is not from on high or from God but from beneath. It is given him from the Devil himself, and his sole purpose is to bring to ruin all that stands for God and truth—to take souls to hell with him with his deceptions, lies, and supposed miracles. He will be worshipped by most of the world because of his seeming wisdom and charismatic personality. Most of the world will see him as the savior and long-awaited hero of mankind. He will promise to alleviate all of the problems of the world, past, present, and future. His subtlety will be absolutely irresistible for most people.

Revelation 13:2 says, "And the dragon gave him his power, and seat, and great authority." In other words, all of the experience, evil knowledge, and power the Devil has gained and can muster will be brought forth in this one man for one brief moment in history. There has never been anything like it, and there never will be again.

But now I'm getting ahead of myself. First there must be a change in world conditions. This change is described most accurately by two prophets, Daniel and John. Revelation 13:1 says, "And I stood upon the sand of the sea, and saw a beast rise up out of the sea, having seven heads and ten horns, and upon his horns, ten crowns, and upon his heads the name of blasphemy."

When it comes to Bible prophecy (or eschatology), God seems to like to use a great deal of symbolism. The beast John is talking about is not a living monster that actually rises up out the sea roaring like Gorgo, dripping wet. It is obvious from the book of Daniel that a beast in this instance is a world system of political power. It is a gathering of nations and kings of the same mind and purpose to gain control of the world (so no one will be left out.).

In chapter 7 of Daniel, he sees a vision of four beasts or world systems that would rise to power far into the future from his time. These four kingdoms are believed to be Greece, Babylon,

Med-Persia, and Rome. The vision of Rome seems to be a dual vision, however. It describes the Roman Empire and the last-days power system of the beast that John saw in Revelation in perfect detail. This does not make his vision a contradiction in terms. What it does mean is that God knew in advance that the Roman Empire and the last days system of the beast were so similar that he could describe them both in one vision. We can compare the two and realize that God has indeed given us a comparison so we can have some idea of what the last-days kingdom is like.

Let's take an actual look at Daniel 7:7:

> After this I saw in the night visions, and behold a fourth beast, dreadful and terrible, and strong exceedingly; and it had great iron teeth; it devoured and break in pieces, and stamped the residue with the feet of it: and it was diverse from all the beasts that were before it; and it had ten horns.

In this verse, we get a more accurate account of what the new system is going to be like. The power and persuasion it will have in its grasp is without a doubt the worst this world has ever seen. It eats anything that challenges it with great iron teeth, and if there is anything left over, it stomps on that with its feet. In this last little sentence, "and it had ten horns" is very significant because it agrees with Revelation 13:1.

We do not have to assume an interpretation of the seventh chapter of Daniel because in verses 15 and 16, he says was grieved in the spirit and asked to know the interpretation and truth of his vision of the beasts. In verse 23, the angel tells Daniel, "Thus he said, the fourth beast shall be the fourth kingdom upon earth, which shall be diverse from all kingdoms and shall devour the whole earth, and shall tread it down, and break it in pieces." The word *diverse* here means different. It gives us the idea that this system will be unlike any other kingdoms that ruled the earth before. It is stronger and much more merciless than its three predecessors. It is dreadful, terrible, and extremely strong.

Turning back to Revelation 13:2, we might now get a clearer understanding of what this bunch of animals means: "And the beast which I saw was like unto a leopard, very fast quick and cunning—and his feet were as the feet of a bear, nothing can challenge it or stand in the way—and his mouth as the mouth of a lion." His mouth speaks great things, and his voice roars like a lion to challenge and put fear in the heart of his enemies and to cause the world to fear his authority.

Daniel 7:24 says, "And the ten horns out of this kingdom are ten kings that shall arise: another shall rise after them; and he shall be diverse from the first, and he shall subdue three kings."

Now, in putting together all we have studied so far, we can come to several conclusions. First, something will happen to change the present world condition of governments. Perhaps a series of events rather than just one will cause the world to consolidate into ten kingdoms and kings that will have absolute power, dominion, and authority over the entire earth. (Many Christian leaders have said that this ten-kingdom government is a more powerful version of the European Common Market. Here again we come to a part where it is possible to speculate many possibilities dealing with the subject of prophecy. It's possible that this new kingdom will be the European Common Market, but I can't really speculate or come up with something to argue this opinion. I feel, however, that this could be very inaccurate.)

Next we see who is really in charge of the operation when we continue to the next sentence of Revelation 13:2: "And the dragon (the devil), gave him his power, his seat, and great authority." The Devil, that age-old serpent who is the culmination of all evil and caused Adam and Eve to fall from grace in the garden of Eden—therefore causing all the woes and misery of mankind that have lasted throughout history—shall give all that he has to this last kingdom. All of his strength and power will be poured into this new leader. In just this one moment in all of time that the earth has been since the beginning until now, Satan is going to pull out all of the stops and bring out his trump card ace and lay it on the table for all the world to see. In his last desperate and final assault on the world, he will believe he can finally triumph against all the Lord God almighty stands for. That's why the Bible keeps saying it is different. Because no dictator on the face of the earth in all history has been given all that Satan has. All of the most horrible dictators and merciless ruthless rulers and dark kingdoms of the past will not hold a candle to this last-ditch effort of Satan to rule the world at last and forever.

Now that the new ruling ten kings have taken over and the system is running smoothly, we'll move down to Daniel 7:8:

> I considered the horns, and, behold, there came
> up among them another little horn, before whom
> there were three of the first plucked up by the
> roots: and, behold, in this were eyes like the eyes
> of man, and a mouth speaking great things.

Now we see the appearance of the antichrist. He is definitely an individual man and not a system or a computer but a man because he is a horn like the other horns and he has the eyes of a man and a mouth speaking great things. We may brag about computers, but I have never heard a machine brag about itself. I mentioned this because I have heard it said that the antichrist could be a computer or an advanced machine of some sort. But as we can see from actual demonstration of Scripture, he cannot possibly be anything other than a man of flesh and blood.

Next he rises to power and takes over the ten-kingdom government. He does it swiftly, and none of the ten kings can stand in his way. We know this because three of the ten kings do not like the challenge and authority the antichrist brings with him, and they are plucked out by their roots and thrown out of their seats. There seems nothing left behind of their respected positions. There doesn't seem to be a mention of a debate or a power struggle here between these three kings and the antichrist. Apparently he simply dethrones them and casts them out. There is no mention of why this happens, though it seems quite significant. Perhaps he doesn't like their looks or something.

The fact of the matter is that they are absolutely powerless to stop him. They are defanged swiftly and quietly and with no regard to whatever influence they may have had from the beginning of their rule. This gives a clear indication of the kind of power and influence the antichrist has at his disposal. There have been rulers, dictators, and presidents who were popular in the past who had the backing of their people or government, but never one of such power and influence as a person coming on the scene with so very little mention of his growth to that position. The new little horn is indeed different from all who were before him.

Now if we were to turn back to Matthew 24, we are given even more agreement and more detail about the time of the antichrist. Verse 15 says, "When ye therefore shall see the abomination of desolation, spoken of by Daniel the prophet, stand in the holy place (Whoso reads, let him understand.)."

In the old Hebrew law, it is understood that any time a non-Jew or Gentile walked into a Jewish sanctuary, it was labeled an abomination. In other words, the Jews were considered the only people who were allowed to enter their own places of worship, and if someone else of another race or national origin walked in, he was desecrating the temple. Jesus is describing just that. The man who is the antichrist may not be a Jew. He may be of some other race or origin. He is not only a desecration but an abomination or turns things from alive and colorful to desert like.

From verses 16 through 20, Jesus says that when the people who live in Judea see the antichrist walk in the temple and take over, to run like mad. He says not to go back to their houses for any reason to get their clothes or anything else. Women who are pregnant will suffer because they will be slowed down and taxed to have the strength to go on. He says, "Pray that your flight not be in the winter nor on the Sabbath day." The old Hebrew traditions were such that you could not venture very far from your home on the Sabbath. If these people who are not going along with the antichrist have to run on the Sabbath, they could become obvious and easily captured. When the antichrist comes to power, many of these old traditions will be brought back.

We can now draw several conclusions. The antichrist may not be of Jewish origin. He is a man of flesh and blood. He will eventually end up in Jerusalem as a ruling figure. And he will be worshipped as a god by most of the world.

If you were to sit down and read the Bible from cover to cover, you would discover that God has given us the gospel through that tiny little nation on the Asian continent. Starting from Moses on down to the last of the Old Testament prophets to Jesus and the epistles to Revelation, he has given us the law and the prophets and the mercy of Christ's death on the cross. Almost all of God's words were written within those little borders. Yet no other book in history has changed the lives of so many people, influenced mighty nations, and presented so great a challenge to our daily lives.

In many counties under dictatorship, the Bible is as illegal as it is to pedal heroin or worse. When dictators take over, Bibles are often the first thing destroyed. No other book in the history of mankind has been talked about, written about, analyzed, criticized, or feared so much as the Bible. No other book has been so loved and hated. No other book has been translated into so many translations and stayed on the bestseller list for all time for as long as it has existed.

It contains a fascinating and marvelous account of a history of people who have been at every station of life. The Jewish people have prospered and starved. They have been right with God, and they have fallen into anarchy and treacherous evil. They have been united in oneness of mind and spirit, and they have fought bloody civil wars.

Finally, in the end they were smitten by the wrath of God and scattered to the far corners of the earth. Only in May of 1948 were they brought back to that little nation—that little plot of land. And try as they may, her enemies have not succeeded at destroying her from off the face of the earth. For 2000 years, the Jewish people were scattered throughout the world and established themselves in other countries and in essence became part of those countries.

God told Moses this would happen and later on Israel would become stiff necked and turn away from him to other gods of rock and metal. But again, God promised in Ezekiel that he would not only bring Israel back together as a nation, but in the book of Romans he also promised that he would bring them to a full knowledge of Jesus Christ as their Savior. As we can see, though, God has fulfilled his promise of bringing the Jews back to their homeland, but he has not yet fulfilled the later part about believing in Christ. But this will certainly be one of the greatest earthly miracles God has ever done besides sending his Son to die on the cross for this dark world.

Satan, therefore, in his attempt to mimic God, will send *his* son the antichrist to Jerusalem to enter the temple of worship and to set himself up as a new god and savior. We must assume at this point then that a new temple, like the one built by Solomon the king so long ago, will be rebuilt in that same city. That old temple is gone, but a new one must be built on or in about the same spot. For the moment, however, a Muslim church is standing on that same spot. I have read reports and heard rumors that the Jews and other experts are speculating that the old temple was really located just a few yards from where the Muslim church is standing now. Whether it is built somewhere else or where the Muslim church (or Dome of the Rock church) is located I will leave up to the expert prophecy teachers. To me it doesn't matter; it will happen regardless.

Here are two more signs of the end that we can look for when these things begin to happen. First, the Jews will be brought to a full knowledge of Jesus Christ. Second, the temple of Solomon will be rebuilt.

How will the antichrist come to power? As well as using outright violence to achieve his ends, Satan also uses lies and deceptions to get the job done. In this case, one of the devices he will use is flattery. Surprisingly, in this instance will not force his way to the throne.

Chapter 11 of Daniel is a most fascinating place to read, although most of it is obscure and hazy to me. Still, though, there is much to be gained from reading it. Verse 21, the last sentence, says, "But he shall come in peaceable and obtain the kingdom by flatteries." And verse 32 says, "And such as do wickedly against the covenant shall he corrupt by flatteries." Here is another method that we should be on guard against. The antichrist will not come with a big sign hanging on his chest saying, *"I am the beast."* He will do everything he can to obscure the warnings of the Bible and the Christians of his day. His use of flatteries is a most disgusting but effective way of getting what he wants. And he will not only flatter his way to the top of the heap among the ten kings, but he will also use this method to keep control of his empire. I'm sure he will expand this to his followers throughout the world also.

If you want to obtain something from someone who is reluctant to give it up whatever it is and you do not want to use brute force, how do you get it? Certainly not by badgering and insulting that person. You tell people what good people they are and what good friends they've been. If someone butters you up with stuff like how handsome you are or how beautiful you are, you're not likely to come back with a harsh response unless you are aware of some underlying motive that proves the flatterer insincere. We can all identify with this method at some time or other in our lives, but we may not be able to recognize it right away when it comes to the antichrist unless we are forewarned to be on guard against it.

His personality will be very enticing and charismatic. He is a human being empowered by all the lies, tricks, and subtleties of the Devil himself. He will be considered to be of superhuman intelligence. He will probably feed the poor and hungry and clothe the naked. He will heal diseases and bring back to life that which was dead. But worst of all, he will bring the dreadful lie of hope for a world starving for hope. But behind all of the good works he uses will be his wretched motivation of darkness and hell.

In essence the antichrist will use the oldest tricks in the book. The complaining preacher in the book of Ecclesiastes says there is nothing new under the sun. The Devil is not on an equal level with God. He is a created being that was once a beautiful angel who plotted to take over the throne of God. He has, of course, failed to do this impossible thing and so was cast down to earth by the Lord's almighty hand. He cannot create something from nothing as God does. He must use what is already available from this creation. He is therefore limited in his power and authority. In the book of Job, we discover that the Devil can do nothing unless God allows it. But it also says, "When the enemy comes in like a flood, the Spirit of the Lord shall lift up a standard against him" (Isa. 59:19). The antichrist will not come to power until the gospel is preached to all the world. He will not come into his position without ample and continuous warning from God not to listen to his lies or worship him.

If we were to really take a close look at the Bible, we would realize that one of its central themes is to turn away from evil and to do good. We must follow the road to salvation, though it be straight and narrow and full of many thorns and hardships, rather than the path of destruction, which is wide and paved with earthly riches. Proverbs 4:14–15 says, "Enter not into the path of the wicked and go not in the way of evil men. Avoid it, pass by it, turn from it, and pass away."

The decision whether to believe in the Word of God or not has been with us since the beginning of time. We do not have to worship the antichrist to end up in hell. The doctrine of Christ has always been quite clear about that. All we have to do is not believe in the only-begotten Son of God, Jesus Christ (Mark 16:16). We are not saved by being good Christians or people or by doing good works (although good works are commendable) such as even the antichrist will do to deceive the world. We are brought into the kingdom of God by faith and simply believing that Christ is real and that he really died on the cross for us and in three days was raised from the dead (Rom. 10:9).

From the moment we receive him into our hearts, we are changed people. Then we are given the desire to be charitable and kind to our fellow man. We are not then motivated by our selfish desires to flatter someone to get what we want. We are less inclined to use and abuse people to our own desirable ends. God can begin to use us for his own good purposes for the betterment of ourselves and others. We look toward God in faith for what we need and what we want and no longer believe that our own pride and strength will see us through the bad times.

As time goes by, the new Christian becomes more knowledgeable and stronger and more mature, and if all goes well, even

Christlike in his or her actions and words. Selfish motives begin to die out, and the love of Jesus Christ begins to shine through. The old, wicked, and sinful self that we once knew begins to fade away, and the new and glorious hope of Jesus begins to become more prominent. Proverbs 4:18 says, "But the path of the just is as the shining light, that shineth more and more unto the perfect day."

I hate to say it, but the antichrist is really the outward embodiment of that old, selfish, sinful self that is within us all. Even if you are the best Christian who has ever lived, you are still at war with the selfish desires that bubble and boil within us all, trying forever to drag us back into the world of sin and condemnation. To be a Christian is to be at war, not only with the Devil and the antichrist but within our own hearts and minds. Our lives are filled and consumed with the constant struggle and tugging of those forces that would persuade us to do one thing or the other. We have to constantly make decisions to do what we know is right or give in to the forces of evil.

But in the struggle, God begins to bring out a new person with the eternal power of his almighty Spirit living within that new man's heart. We may cringe when we have heard about the awful things man has done, such as the horror of Hitler and his gas chambers and the many destructions of violent and evil men. Even so, there is a Hitler that lives within us all. This is why the antichrist is so dangerous—because of his flatteries, lies, and subtleties, especially his flatteries. The one thing he will use to appeal to that little Hitler within us all. The temptation to give in and follow him to destruction will be there for every one of us on the face of the earth, Christian and non-Christian alike. That decision has always been with us. It will just be more obvious, and no one will be able to put it off any more. We will no longer be able to sit on the fence and bide our time. The trigger of the gun of the Lord's almighty hand of justice will already be pulled and the hammer falling. We will have to decide whether to get shot or jump out of the way.

I remember reading a book (*When Being Jewish Was a Crime*) a while back about a Jewish man who received Jesus into his heart and became a Christian in Poland just before World War II. He was converted to Christianity by Jewish Christians. After the war broke out, he found himself in and out of Warsaw (a ghetto used by the Nazis to store Jews for later execution) and experiencing and observing all the horrors of the Nazi campaign to wipe out the Jews. Time and time again, he was miraculously saved from capture and death. His ending testimony was both shocking and sad, however. He said that when he went back to the many Christian churches that once cared for him, he found that quite a few of them had taken sides with Hitler! And they were not only turning Jews away but were also turning them over to the Nazis! These were Bible-believing, Spirit-filled, born-again, etc., Christian churches. What a terrible and tragic event!

Another even braver man by the name of Dietrich Bonhoeffer who was a German Lutheran pastor stood against Hitler and the persecution of the Jews throughout the war. In the end, Hitler had him hung, but he found out exactly the same thing. Most of the church had either taken sides with the Nazis or were sorely afraid to stand against them. Dietrich once said, "I am a Christian first and foremost, a German second. And I can only hope to God that the two will never oppose each other." But of course they met head on in a terrible life-and-death struggle. Dietrich was one of the few shining lights in the midst of thick darkness, but his struggle shows us the truth of what will most likely be in the future. Very few will stand for truth in the end.

In our own day and age, the church feels as if it is immune to doing something similar to the German churches. But let's take a look at Luke 21:16: "And you shall be betrayed by both parents and brethren, kinfolk and friends, and some of you shall they cause to be put to death." The antichrist will not be a distant dictator of some foreign country as in the past. What is going to happen here is right in our own homes, businesses, and backyards. Let's take a look at Revelation 13:4, 7:

> And they worshipped the dragon which gave power unto the beast: and they worshipped the beast, saying, who is like unto the beast? Who is able to make war with him? ... And all that dwell upon the earth shall worship him, whose names are not written in the book of the life of the Lamb slain from the foundation of the earth.

In other words, if a person is not a sincere Christian he or she will end up worshipping the antichrist. We see here that God is going to separate good from evil during this time, and it will only be too obvious whose side the individual is on.

In the beginning of the book of Daniel, we read that there was a king by the name of Nebuchadnezzar. He ruled over a great empire called Babylon. This great empire came on the scene because Israel had fallen into deep sin, and God was about to use this evil nation to bring severe judgment on Israel. It wasn't as if this came as a big surprise—at least not to the folks who still believed in and followed God. The prophets had been warning Israel to repent and turn back to God for a long time—many years, in fact. King Jehoiakim came from a good bloodline his, father being King Josiah. But Jehoiakim was apparently unaffected by his father's influence and continued during his reign to lead the Israelites into deep sin, which God was not at all pleased with.

God warned, and one day he drew the line, and Babylon rose up as a mighty nation like a streak of lightning in the sky. Nebuchadnezzar easily conquered Israel and marched with his powerful army into Judah. But then he got word that his father had died, so he left the city and left Jehoiakim in charge. During this time, Jehoiakim got a brilliant (actually not-so-brilliant) idea. He decided to make an alliance with the Egyptians to attack back at Babylon and gain back Israel's freedom.

This is when God called the prophet Jeremiah and explained to him that he needed to tell the king not to try and make this alliance with Egypt because Israel was under judgment and Babylon was able to conquer them only because God allowed it. But would Jehoiakim listen? No! Not at all. In fact, he had Jeremiah jailed for telling the great king things he just didn't want to hear. But Jeremiah summoned a scribe and had word sent to the people that because of this alliance, terrible judgment would fall on the king and his court. Alas, though, when Jehoiakim got the message, he ripped it up with a knife and threw it into the fireplace. This riled the Lord to extreme anger, and when Nebuchadnezzar got wind of the alliance, he swooped down and invaded again, this time leaving the king and his court laying outside speared, dead, and bleeding in the streets.

Then he took a portion of the best or the cream of the crop of Israel—that is the scholars, athletes, and accomplished and successful people to Babylon—to serve under him. He also took many of the temple treasures and placed them in his own temple to be articles for his own god. Daniel was among these folks. While Daniel was with the king in Babylon, some incredible things happened. He was visited by angels and given great prophecies of the coming of Christ into the world for the first time and great prophecies and visions of the powerful empires that would rise and fall. But he also told about the end times, from which we can derive some windows into what the end will really be like. It's funny how Daniel completely agrees with the book of Revelation.

During this time, another significant event also occurred—the plight of Shadrach, Meshach, and Abednego. Nebuchadnezzar decided to make an image that was to be worshipped by everyone, but these three men told the king to his face that they would not worship this image because they believed in the God of their fathers only and that to worship any other would be a terrible betrayal. Nebuchadnezzar became furious, fired up a monstrous furnace, and told his servants to make it seven times hotter than normal. In fact, the furnace was so hot it killed those servants when they approached it to throw in the three. They said they would stand their ground whether God delivered them from the flames or not.

But when they landed in the furnace, God protected them, and they were untouched by the flames. The king was astonished, as the Bible puts it, because when he went closer to the furnace, he not only saw that the three men were not hurt by the flames, but he also saw someone like the Son of God walking around in there with them. He then called to them and they came out, and he decreed that no one could be dishonorable to their God or they would face severe penalties. How could Nebuchadnezzar have known that the person walking around in the furnace was the Son of God? The only way he could have known was that God revealed it to him in his mysterious way.

But then Nebuchadnezzar became very foolish in his heart and was very arrogant and thought very much of himself, so God took away his reason. He went out and ate grass like an animal and grew nails like a bird's claws. God did this to show him and others just who is really in charge.

After this humbling, his son, Belshazzar, took the throne and became an even more arrogant and self-worshipping ruler. In chapter 5, we find him having a great feast and drinking wine from the cups stolen from the Jewish temple. He was in the midst of worshipping gods of wood and brass, iron, and stone.

But in the middle of his feast, he noticed a mysterious hand writing something on the wall across from him. He couldn't read the writing, so he called in his best astrologers and wise men, and they couldn't interpret it either. The queen, however, knew about Daniel and his past successes at interpreting dreams and visions, so the king called him in to tell him what it meant. He must have been pretty scared because this chapter says that he was so nervous his knees were knocking and he was breathing hard.

Daniel told Belshazzar that he knew very well all that had taken place with his father and that he had no business ignoring the true God of the universe. He told the king that he was debasing God by drinking from the stolen cups of the temple and worshipping other gods (gods that can neither talk nor walk nor see nor hear). Daniel went on to say that the handwriting said, "MENE MENE TEKEL Upharsin." God has numbered the days of your kingdom and finished it. You have been weighed in the balance and found wanting (wanting meaning you have left much to be desired). Your kingdom will be divided and handed over to the Medes and the Persians. And of course, that is exactly what happened. As far as historians can tell, this was the real condition of Babylon in those days.

During the time of Israel's captivity in Babylon, another prophet showed up, and his name was Ezekiel. God sent him to encourage the Jews even in their miserable circumstances. *God did not abandon his people even though they were backsliding and under judgment.* This shows the tremendous grace of God as the Bible does throughout history. *Foxe's Book of Martyrs* says that Ezekiel was dragged behind a cart until his head burst open. This shows that the prophets loved their country and its people enough to die for them.

Ezekiel had awesome visions of heavenly beings. Manny UFO enthusiasts have tried to interpret these visions as space vehicles showing up in ancient history. But most of those who study the Bible closely realize that God was showing Ezekiel and Israel a piece of heaven to encourage them and to show them he was still hanging on to them as he promised in Scripture. This should be a great encouragement to all Christians of today, whether we are backsliding or not. It took tremendous commitment on the part of Ezekiel to have the courage and the will to give Israel these visions. It also shows that God does not forsake his people even during the great tribulation. The Bible indicates that there will be Christians around during this time, and they and we in our time can take heart that God is still in the saving and encouraging business.

The bottom line to all of this is the central theme that runs through all Scripture, and that is it's not wise to ignore God, especially when he has given fair and constant warning. It all started with Israel continuing in deep sin. Some theologians say they were even sacrificing babies to other gods in temple ceremonies. God was very patient with them and put up with their nonsense far longer than any human being would have. Many folks seem to have a negative image of God as the angry man in the sky with a lightning bolt in one hand and a hammer in the other, just waiting to pounce on someone for breaking one of his laws. But a closer examination of the Bible reveals a much different picture. He is a just God, yes, but also a very patient and loving God who is willing to be our friend even when we fail miserably to live up to his standards. The story of Ezekiel is a very encouraging event because it shows us quite definitely that God loves us despite our major shortcomings.

A few years ago when I first starting writing this book, I was praying before I went to bed (I do that occasionally), and I asked the Lord to reveal more to me about the antichrist and what he would be like.

That night I dreamed I was inside a small room that was jam-packed with people from all parts of the globe. There were old people and young, rich and poor, and women and children. Suddenly there appeared a young man at the only door that would allow an exit. I remember saying to myself that he was a good-looking young man who was neatly dressed and had good manners. He was a little different from the other people in the room, but how I just couldn't quite put my finger on how.

The young man became a fascination because he began to speak, though he was obscure and melted in with the crowd before the whole room became silent to hear all of the marvelous things he was saying. When the whole room became silent, some people sat down, so I sat down beside a little girl who was probably about seven or eight years old.

Two things happened almost simultaneously. The little girl beside me suddenly blurted out so everyone could hear, "He's the antichrist!" Few people believed it, but at the same moment she said this, the young man pulled out from behind him an M-16 rifle. I was paralyzed with fear, but I managed to stand up somehow. Just as I stood up, the young man began firing his weapon on automatic. He kept yelling and repeating that if anyone took their eyes from him, they would certainly die. I kept my eyes glued on him myself.

He took no thought for anyone. He killed old people, women, and children in a murderous, merciless rage. People were screaming and running, but there was no place to go; he was blocking the only exit. Finally I decided I had had enough. When he was looking and shooting in another direction, I grabbed the gun from him. Knowing how to operate an M-16 from the army, I dropped the clip and looked at it. There were only three bullets left. I quickly jammed the clip back into the gun, set the selector switch on semi-automatic, and fired the three bullets into the man. Two of the bullets landed square in his head and one in his chest. I saw his blood splatter against the wall behind him. But to my amazement, it only stunned him. I was shocked and confused, but before I could figure out what had happened, the scene changed.

I found myself walking down a long corridor of what I knew was a prison. I finally ended up in a room dimly lit and bland, everything in gray and drab colors. The atmosphere of that room was so oppressive I could hardly stand it. When I looked around, I saw a man standing behind a desk, and I knew he was the warden or the jailer. When I turned back around, I saw the young man standing in a cell behind bars about an arm's length from me.

I asked the young man, "Why don't you repent?"

He just smiled, looked at me with contempt, and said, "You know I can't do that."

Suddenly I knew the little girl was right. He was the antichrist! I also knew then that to think I could stop him with carnal weapons like guns was vanity. The incident in the room came clear to me then. I knew the antichrist would be killed and then raised from the dead as in Revelation 13:3: "And I saw one of his heads as it were wounded to death; and his deadly wound was healed." It also came to me that he was nothing more than a murderer and a criminal. He would be the worst human being that ever lived. He cared for nothing except his own selfish desires and ambitions to take over the world. I hated him.

I heard the jailer behind the desk say that they were going to let him out. I became angry and yelled at him that this man was the antichrist and a murderer. I told him that I was one of the few people who were left from that room who witnessed his killing of innocent women and children with my own eyes. The jailer just laughed and told me that this could not possibly be and that the young man in there was only being held for questioning. He was known in the community as a good person and was a well-respected and fine, upstanding citizen of the community.

The scene changed again, and I was standing in a long corridor watching from a distance. The jailer was releasing the young man from the cell. As he was talking to the jailer, the young man turned and began walking toward me. His steps were slow and deliberate. The corridor was long, and he had quite a distance to walk to get to me.

Then a strange thing happened. As he got further down the hall, he turned into a sort of metal robot. Then he began to grow bigger and taller. It made some sort of strange vibrating noise as it grew taller and bigger with each step until it broke the ceiling of the hallway and its stature became so huge that its head shot up through the clouds and out of sight. I was absolutely filled with fear, but there was no place to run.

Finally the monster was only a few feet away. I knew I was powerless to stop it, and I knew it intended to put me through a most excruciating death. With almost no hope or strength left within me, I fell to my knees and cried, "Jesus!" But my voice was almost too weak to eke out even that one word. Suddenly there was a sound like thunder, which I recognized as the voice of God. When I looked up from my fearful and bowed-head position, the monster was reduced to a toy robot almost three feet high. It was babbling ridiculous obscenities at me and God. I began to laugh and rejoice. I told him to be gone before he invoked the fierce anger of the Lord. He turned and ran as fast as he could. By now a handful of people had gathered in the room, and they watched him run shamefully by them in fear of the Lord. I knew these were the people who helped bring him to power. They watched with disgust and confusion as he turned into a toy and ran.

The only reason the system of the antichrist becomes so powerful is because people fear him and give him his power. The Word of God has never exalted the antichrist. It says that he exalts himself. I hope my reader will pause here and realize this one fact because it is so important. It is only because men allow other men to take an exalted position that such men become exalted. Hitler entered into his position of political power because of only one vote. I have heard it said, and it is true, that the only way for evil men to take over is for good men to lay down and do nothing.

Next the antichrist will come to power through the disguise of religion. For many people, I suppose this would seem a contradiction in terms. However, in the light of our present-day situation, it is not. Since God has given his Word and a conscience to man, humans have perverted and rationalized it to get around the truth of the matter that all human beings are born sinners since the fall of Adam and Eve in the garden of Eden. We just can't seem to deal with the reality of sin in our lives.

Knowing Jesus Christ as he really is and having him live inside your heart is not a religion at all. The church should not be a religion but a living, breathing organism set upon the living reality of Jesus Christ today. To be born-again is not only an intellectual decision. It is a heartfelt spiritual awakening deep within the deepest and darkest corners of the soul. It is a complete turnaround from the dark road of destruction and hell that a man was once on to the road of salvation, heaven, and eternal life.

God never meant for us to nitpick and tear at one another's beliefs until we had thousands of different religions and denominations. But the sad fact of the matter is that there are so many different religions. To the average man, it can be as confusing and strange as stepping onto another planet in some far-off galaxy or watching a political talk show on Sunday, whichever comes first.

Chapter 17 of Revelation indicates that all of the dead, false, corrupt, and reeking religions that have said they believe in God but have absolutely nothing to do with them in their hearts and even in their actions will all be gathered in one heart and in one place, and they will give rise to the antichrist.

It would be nice if I could quote the whole seventeenth chapter, but I'm afraid of putting my reader to sleep, so I will skip down to verse 3 in the second clause: "And I saw a woman sit upon a scarlet coloured beast full of the names of blasphemy, having seven heads and ten horns."

We already know that the seven heads and ten horns are the new system of political power that will rise after our future change of world conditions. The seven heads and ten horns are a complete political power in and of themselves. So who is this wretched woman riding on a purple blob? Verse 4 says:

> And the woman was arrayed in purple and
> scarlet colour, and decked with gold and precious
> stones and pearls, and having a golden cup in her
> hand full of abominations and filthiness of her
> fornication:

If we don't try to read too much into this verse, we can see that we simply have a woman who is symbolic of something terrible. She is decked out with all of the earthly pleasures and riches, and her cup of these sinful pleasures is filled to the brim. Verse 5 says

> And upon her forehead was a name written, MYSTERY, BABYLON THE GREAT, THE MOTHER OF HARLOTS AND ABOMINATIONS OF THE EARTH.

The use of the "GREAT MOTHER OF HARLOTS" is what makes me think that God is talking about a guise of religion. He often referred to the nation of Israel as whorish when they fell away from him and began to give favors to nations who should have been their enemies. He considered this a nation that committed fornication or immoral sex with its enemies. Thus we have a church, which once knew God and indeed was once his finest and most trustworthy organization, which has with time eroded into a dead and false religion. This religion is cloaked with a few good works to make it the ultimate example of the worst kind of hypocrisy.

There are already clergy and political leaders working toward an ecumenical movement to unite certain organizations and denominations in cooperation to become one in mind in spirit. I believe this organization is called the World Council of Churches or WCC for short. It is definitely a liberal organization and very dangerous to the world, at least spiritually. There is another reason for the harlot church's motivation, however. Verse 6 says:

> And I saw the woman drunken with the blood of the saints, and with the blood of the martyrs of

Jesus: and when I saw her, I wondered with great admiration.

The harlot church will not only lust after political power and ride on the already established power of the ten kings but will also fight against the true church of Jesus Christ with outright violence and murder. In this cause the beast or the ten kingdoms and the Mother Harlot will be in one accord. This is to stamp out the real gospel of Jesus and to establish their own manmade religion, which will probably ultimately worship the antichrist.

But the harlot's worship of the antichrist will almost certainly lead to its total destruction. Verse 16 says:

> And the ten horns which thou sawest upon the beast, these shall hate the whore, and shall make her desolate and naked, and shall eat her flesh and burn her with fire.

If we look at verse 17, we can see that God's wrath has burned against the harlot, and he satisfies his anger by allowing these two conspirators of evil to turn against one another. Unfortunately for the harlot, it is a lost battle. This should give us another insight into the true nature of the antichrist. He is now a betrayer of those who were once his friends and those who helped him gain political clout.

> For God hath put in their hearts to fulfill his will, and to agree, and give their kingdom unto the beast, until the words of God shall be fulfilled. (Rev. 17:17)

Now we have one more verse to talk about from the book of Daniel.

> And after the league made with him he shall
> work deceitfully: for he shall come up, and shall
> become strong with a small people. (Dan. 11:23)

In my dream, I mentioned a small group of people who I knew helped the antichrist come to power. It is from these people that he draws his strength and encouragement to go on. This is another sign that we can look for in the rise of the antichrist. Another important sign we can look for in the rise of the antichrist comes from Revelation 13:5-6

> And there was given unto him a mouth speaking
> great things and blasphemies; and power was
> given unto him to continue forty and two
> months. And he opened his mouth in blasphemy
> against God, to blaspheme his name, and his
> tabernacle, and them that dwell in heaven.

As I stated before, the antichrist is the embodiment of all that is evil and against God. He is the antichrist. Therefore he will not recognize God's sovereign power over mankind and over the creation. He will try to belittle God and make him the object of scorn and ridicule. In doing this, he will actually go so far as to blaspheme God and curse him and claim to be more powerful. He does this to put down the almighty, powerful God so he can exalt himself in the eyes of the world.

If you've ever sat back and wondered why people actually gossip, you would find that they do this to put down the person they are talking about to exalt themselves or make themselves feel better. This, in my opinion, is the rationale of the antichrist. He will praise himself and attack God the Father, the Son, and the Holy Spirit to accomplish his murderous will against all the things of God. Why? Because he knows deep inside that this is not the case. He knows that God has ultimately defeated him at the cross. He knows that God is all powerful and sovereign and that the Holy Spirit is all knowing. He knows that his evil, sinful, wicked deeds will be brought to the light on the day he is cast into the lake of fire, where he will stay forever. He is in no way a challenge to God's matchless power and throne. Indeed, God laughs at the wicked man, for he knows his day is coming (Ps. 37:13).

There is a contradiction that lies within the antichrist, which is his worst weakness. He has convinced himself that he is a god of some sort—that he is more powerful than the Lord and he can accomplish the monumental task of taking over His throne. Yet he knows this thought is pure folly and laughable, for God is the source of all creation. So he overruns himself in trying to compensate for his fear of the wrath of an angry, invincible God who is counting his days. According to Revelation 11:2, this is forty-two months or three and one half years from the time he enters the temple in Jerusalem and proclaims that he is God. At least that is what I derive from Revelation 11:2 since it says that the Gentiles (or non-Jews) will tread Jerusalem underfoot for that amount of time.

This is when the world can take warning and realize what the antichrist really is—a liar. Because he himself knows that he is dreadfully in trouble with God and his time is short. In this way, he actually recognizes Christ as the only true redeemer. He sees that God cannot be defeated, so he hides behind empty curses that cannot alter the destiny, the purpose, or the mind of God one breath or one hair. He is doomed for damnation and misery for all eternity, and he knows it.

> And it was given unto him to make war with the saints, and to overcome them: and power was given him over all kindred's, and tongues, and nations. (Rev. 13:7)

This verse is usually ignored or rationalized away by most Bible teachers and prophecy teachers and not without reason. Unfortunately, much of Christianity has fallen into a dark and dangerous pit of materialism and escapism, which has built up a wall around it that is almost impenetrable. Many have forgotten that our most important priority is to persuade those around us to believe in Jesus and in the things of God. As a result, the flame of golden candlestick on the altar of God has burned low and weak. It is failing to light the hearts of those in terrible darkness and despair. And I think their attitudes have lulled them into a comfortable place of false security and given them a worldly ambition to seek after only those temporary things.

The systematic and well-organized attack of the antichrist will therefore catch most Christians off guard. The verses I have repeated from Luke 21 indicate that the very people with whom one lives will become his most severe enemies and turn that Christian over to be imprisoned and in some cases put to death. If the average Christian has not become more than average by then and become a seeker of the Word of God, then he or she will most certainly be swept away by the hurricane and powerful tide of oncoming events.

The subject of the doctrine of the rapture is one I hate, but here goes. If the reader has never heard of the rapture, you will want to read these next words because I am sure you will hear about it again. There is a belief in many churches that long before the great troubles I have just described will come upon the earth, all sincere and born-again Christians will be caught away and disappear from the face of the earth to dwell with Christ until his final second return. Cars and airplanes will crash as a result. The world will be stunned at this strange event of a large number of people having disappeared from the world.

In all fairness, it is possible that there will be a taking out or a pre-tribulation rapture before the judgment of God falls on the world. However, close examination of Scripture does not really reveal a definite timeline for this event. The word *rapture* never really occurs in the Bible. But there is mention of a taking away. Actually, the rapture, upon close examination, turns out to be only a theory. There are actually three theories on the subject: pre-, mid-, and post-tribulation rapture. To me the Bible seems to preach all three. We must keep in mind that our opinion about the rapture has nothing to do with our salvation. We must also keep in mind that this event will occur when God wants it to no matter what anyone believes about it. Our opinion about it will not change God's mind in any way, shape, or form.

Through all the ages, the church of Christ has been attacked from the time of the earliest church to the Roman Empire, who killed Christians for sport and threw them to the lions. This happens in our time, where godless dictators imprison and kill people for simply owning a Bible or holding a prayer meeting. How is that Christians of our day in America have come to the conclusion that we are exempt from severe trials and persecutions like our ancestral brothers and sisters in Christ endured? Again, it is the rise toward materialism and with it taking for granted our religious freedom in the United States. The comfort of America has pacified much of Christianity into a sense of false security. The result is a bookshelf full of books and masses of preachers and teachers crying, "All is well! All is well!" The truth is that not only is everything not well but on the very brink of war and destruction.

I personally believe that God would have been more open in his description of what is going to happen if the pre-tribulation rapture is really to occur. Most of the Scriptures that Christians point out that we will be swept away are in reference to the resurrection on the day of judgment or they are in the wrong place, such as at the end of Matthew 24. Or they are too hazy because they are taken out of context. However, this can be an endless controversy, and it creates more friction and heat than it does light, so we will leave this theory behind and move on

Regardless of our differences, it is the individual Christian and the little church on the corner or those who meet in homes that will have the greatest impact on their community or even the world. The only person who can decide which side to be on is the individual. No one can make up his mind for him. The forces that be may try to persuade, but it is always up to the individual to make his or her decision as to which way to go. I always hope it will be to follow Christ.

Weapons of Violence

> He that leadeth into captivity shall go into captivity: he that killeth with the sword must be killed with the sword. Here is the faith and patience and the faith of the saints. (Rev. 13:10)

In reference to my dream, I realized that it is useless to fight against the antichrist with weapons of violence. Zechariah 4:6b says, "Not by might, nor by power, but by my spirit, saith the Lord of hosts." There are small factions of Christians who have decided that we will go through the tribulation but have also decided to abandon the doctrine of faith by building up arms, building up food, and digging fallout shelters. If we could only grasp the teachings of Christ that we do not have to fight our enemies with guns and violence. He alone is the judge, and we are victorious through the cross, not by shooting our assailants. I leave the shooting and killing to the bad guys and shy away from it in the practice of my daily living. We already know that the antichrist will only be on his throne as long as God will allow—no longer and no shorter. No man can change the will of God in this kind of situation. We cannot use ordinary, worldly weapons to fight a spiritual battle.

The False Prophet

> And I beheld another beast coming up out of the
> earth; and he had two horns like a lamb and he
> spake as a dragon. (Rev. 13:11)

There is another evil conspirator who is apparently the assistant
of the antichrist.

Revelation 13:13 says, "And he doeth great wonders, so that he
maketh fire come down from heaven on earth in the sight of
men."

As I have stated before, Satan has been preparing the world for
the appearance of the antichrist for centuries. Our media is full
of the occult and mysticism. By the time the antichrist and his
assistant appear, the world will be fully ready to accept these
satanic miracles and embrace them as a sign that humankind is
evolving into a new era and a new state. I'm sure many will claim
this is the next step in human evolution, and many will probably
have acquired occultic powers themselves. Unfortunately, these
occultic powers will be from the wrong source and will only help
to drag the world into heavier darkness. What do these flashy
miracles do except make a person swoon? They are pretty but
lead to nowhere but that heavy darkness. Verse 14 says:

> And deceiveth them that dwell on the earth by
> the means of those miracles which he had power
> to do in the sight of the beast; saying to them
> that dwell on the earth, that they should make

an image to the beast, which had the wound by
the sword and did live.

Finally the false prophet decides to talk to the worshippers of
the antichrist and tells them that they should make some kind
of image or statue of him to worship also. Here is also the second
reference to the idea that the antichrist will be wounded unto
death yet will live. The first reference says, "Who is like unto
the beast? And who is able to make war with him?" (Rev. 13:4).

This is another way the antichrist will come to power. It is
obvious that most everyone will know about him and actually
then begin to worship him with a bursting forth of praise and
admiration. I don't know how this resurrection works as far as
the powers that be except that it will be from the wrong source
again. Satan is limited in his power, but he does have some.
We can just about imagine the tremendous impact of such a
dramatic event. It will certainly point attention to him and may
even be the single most important event that will raise him up
out of obscurity.

The false prophet is the assistant and friend of the antichrist.
He will no doubt predict the total destruction of God and
Christianity. I'm sure he will be the main perpetrator of the
idea that mankind has evolved into a new era and is becoming
more advanced by way of the mind and its magnificent powers.
The mesmerizing effect of the false prophet and the antichrist
together will probably have a terrible hypnotic effect on
its followers, just as today false doctrine and teachers have
a dark power over theirs. Once a person has fallen mentally

and emotionally into this trap of darkness, it would be very difficult to pull them out. I don't think it will be impossible until that person has received the mark of the beast as described in Revelation 13, but it will be very improbable. We must remember that the world and the harlot church are under God's judgment and believing a lie because they refuse to love the truth.

The Mark of the Beast

> And he causeth all, both small and great, rich and poor, free and bond, to receive a mark in their right hand, or in their foreheads: And that no man might buy or sell, save he that had the mark, or the name of the beast, or the number of his name. Here is wisdom. Let him that hath understanding count the number of the beast: for it is the number of a man and his number is Six hundred threescore and six. (Rev. 13:16–18)

Second Thessalonians 2 makes it quite plain that the antichrist will march into the newly built temple and claim to be God. Satan has obviously been working on the world for a very long time and has gotten a major portion of the population to believe in the paranormal, new-age belief systems and in the occult. The world therefore will not have a problem adoring the antichrist and the false prophet. But the antichrist will not yet be satisfied. He wants all of the hearts and minds of the people, so he requires a mark of allegiance to be put on their foreheads or on their hands to symbolize that a person has given over everything to him and Satan.

The unbelieving world has not always come right out and said that they hate God with a great passion, but it has always been there. All of the concepts I have talked about, from relativity to political correctness to evolution, have all been sacred cows to the unbelieving populace through the ages. Atheism and agnosticism have been the call of the day for thousands of years. When it boils down to true reality, this dark world has been worshipping Satan since the beginning of time but has not really come out and said it in no uncertain terms.

But look at what is happening now during the tribulation. Those who have always loved Satan and hated God can now express their point of view in an open forum. They can call for the death of those who will not cooperate and believe, like they do, that Satan should rule the world and the universe because he has made more sense than God and is more desirable than Christ. Finally, now they have their dark way and can express it in all fullness.

No one can buy or sell without the mark of allegiance. As we can see in Satan's realm, he leaves the world with little choice. Either you take the mark or you die from starvation and homelessness. It becomes a mystery at this point as to why the world would worship the very incarnation of evil at the very cost of one's personal freedom. At one time, at least part of the world would have gone to a miserable death rather than give up the freedoms that once existed, especially in America. But something has changed drastically in this new world of trouble. Satan has captured the minds and hearts of most everyone through his craftiness and subtle deceit. Perhaps at this point most people don't care and would follow the new regime even if they knew they were being deceived.

> For the mystery of iniquity doth already work: only he who now letteth will let, until he be taken out of the way. And then shall the Wicked be revealed, whom the Lord shall consume with the spirit of his mouth, and shall destroy with the brightness of his coming: Even him, whose coming is after the working of Satan with all power and signs and lying wonders, and with all deceivableness of unrighteousness in them that perish; because they received not the love of the truth, that they might be saved. And for this cause God shall send them strong delusion, that they should believe a lie: That they all might be damned who believe not the truth, but had pleasure in unrighteousness. (2 Thess. 2:7–12)

As we can see, the Bible says the mystery of iniquity is already working in the world. We have already discussed many ways Satan is working in the world to bring about the end times and the takeover of the antichrist. The Lord has already said in Daniel, Revelation, and 2 Thessalonians that he is going to destroy the antichrist and all of his works at his second coming. But what is interesting here is the reason given for God allowing the antichrist to come to power in the first place. He sends them strong delusion because they don't love the truth.

This is a very interesting verse because I think it applies to the present-day church in many ways. So many folks these days go to church and sing and jump for joy, but when it comes to the real truth of God's Word, they put up their hands and say, "No thanks, I'm happy and comfortable. Please don't confuse me with the facts." The word of faith and latter rain movements (counterfeit revival) are the greatest examples of this.

There will be no sitting on the fence at this place and time. It will be only too obvious which side you are on. It will be quite obvious if a person is carrying the mark of the beast. Even if it is invisible, it will be obvious that this person has total social acceptance and can buy and sell and keep his or her job. What will not be immediately obvious to those who have taken the mark is the fact that in so doing, they will reap the terrible consequences of the wrath of God.

> And the third angel followed them, saying with a loud voice, If any man worship the beast and his image, and receive his mark in his forehead, or in his hand, the same shall drink of the wine of the wrath of God, which is poured out without mixture into the cup of his indignation: and he shall be tormented with fire and brimstone in the presence of the holy angels, and in the presence of the Lamb: And the smoke of their torment ascendeth up for ever and ever: and they have no rest day nor night, who worship the beast, and his image, and whosoever recieveth the mark of

his name. Here is the patience of the saints: here
are they that keep the commandments of God
and the faith of Jesus. (Rev. 14:9–12)

I don't think social acceptance is quite worth the terrible
judgments that follow the space of time that people accept the
mark of the beast and begin worshipping him. For a short time,
those who worship the antichrist will experience peace. But
then God wakes up and like a sleeping lion begin to roar and to
bring justice upon a world in rebellion against him.

Flying Demons

It seems almost impossible that such incredible and hideous
things should occur even during the time of the great tribulation.
But the book of Revelation is part of God's Word, and if God
is truly telling us what is really going to happen, then these
incredible things will certainly take place. Revelation 8:13 says
that an angel (the older KJV says this is an eagle) was flying
through heaven, "saying woe, woe, woe unto those who inhabit
the earth by reason of the other voices of the trumpet of the
three angels, which are yet to sound."

Chapter 9 of Revelation says that the fifth angel sounded and a
star fell from heaven (probably an angel), and he was given the
key to the bottomless pit. And when he opened the pit, a great
smoke came out, and this smoke was so strong it obscured the
light of the sun. Revelation describes the beings that come out
of this pit:

And the shapes of the locusts were like unto horses prepared unto battle; and on their heads were as it were crowns like gold, and their faces were as the faces of men. 8and they had hair as the hair of women, and their teeth were as the teeth of lions. And they had breastplates, as it were breastplates of iron; and the sound of their wings as the sound of chariots of many horses running to battle. And they had tails like unto scorpions and there stings in their tails: and their power was to hurt men five months. (Rev. 9:7–10)

I find it very interesting that the Bible gives us such vivid detail of these hideous beings. It tells us almost exactly what they look like, and it describes what they can do to humans and for how long. I have heard many folks say that the book of Revelation is full of metaphors and visions that are very cloudy and spiritual and that anyone can attach whatever meaning they want to it. But it seems to me that this chapter, among others, is quite clear about what is going to happen and why.

This is a very interesting question as to why God would send such a terrible and some may say cruel judgment on the earth. These creatures seem the ultimate of terror, worse than our worst nightmares and as terrible as any torture chamber ever devised. But the last verse of this chapter answers that question very well, I believe. Verse 21 says, "Neither repented they of their murders, or of their sorceries, nor of their fornication, nor of their thefts."

I have already discussed much of what is leading up to the judgments and wrath of God in the very tribulation itself. As 2 Thessalonians 3 states, humans have become lovers of themselves. They are selfish and self-centered. They have very little or no conscience about any of their actions. They have allowed Satan's belief systems and doctrines to take over and become the guideline of their whole lifestyle.

We have today witchcraft disguised as "wicca." Kids are dressed in "goth" and run around in dark attire to be part of a growing attitude of worship and love for the Devil. Spiritualism is also popular (also known as necromancy, which is conjuring up the dead for communication). As far as the Bible is concerned, both communication with the dead and reincarnation are put to rest as invalid because of Hebrews 9:27: *"And it is appointed unto men once to die, but after this the judgment."*

In these last days, people have gotten to the point of such depravity that they are practicing full-out witchcraft (probably disguised as something else), as well as worshipping demons and the antichrist, which is the ultimate of idolatry. They are murdering not only each other but also those who refuse to join their evil escapades, so God has sent a terrible judgment on them of equal terror. This judgment will make them and the rest of creation realize that there is no equal to his matchless power, and his justice is absolutely perfect.

Jesus made reference to a time when he saw Satan fall like lightning to the earth. Satan was a beautiful angel and a leader of angels. But pride welled up inside his heart, and he wanted to be God. But that is, of course, impossible. God is the Lord God almighty. He has all the complete attributes that are what makes him God. He is all-powerful. Therefore, it is completely impossible that some created being, such as Satan, could in some kind of rebellion, take over the throne. Let's take a look at Isaiah 14:12–16:

> How art thou fallen from heaven O Lucifer, son of the morning! how art thou cut down to the ground, which didst weaken the nations! For thou hast said in thine heart, I will ascend into heaven, I will exalt my throne above the stars of God: I will sit also upon the mount of the congregation, in the sides of the north: I will ascend above the heights of the clouds; I will be like the Most High. Yet thou shalt be brought down to hell, to the sides of the pit. They that see thee shall narrowly look upon thee, and consider thee saying, Is this the man that made the earth to tremble, that did shake kingdoms;

Revelation 12:4 says, "And his tail drew the third part of the stars of heaven, and did cast them to the earth." I believe that this particular Scripture is referring to the time when Satan rebelled against God, but Satan was able to convince one-third of the angels of heaven to follow him, so they were also cast down to earth with him. These are the demons that follow Satan and do his bidding. They are very probably highly organized in a military fashion. Some are more powerful and have higher rank and responsibility than others (generals, captains, sergeants, privates etc.). I would venture to say that these demons from the bottomless pit are some from the former fall, or they are some kind of creature that God created for this particular purpose and judgment and day and hour.

> And there came out of the smoke locusts upon the earth: and unto them was given power, as the scorpions of the earth have power. And it was commanded them that they should not hurt the grass of the earth, neither any green thing, neither any tree; but only those men which have not the seal of God in their foreheads. And to them it was given that they should not kill them, but that they should be tormented five months: and their torment was as the torment of a scorpion, when he striketh a man. And in those days shall men seek death, and shall not find it; and shall desire to die, and death shall flee from them. (Rev. 9:3–6)

This is an interesting comment in verse 6, saying that they shall seek death in those days and shall not find it. Is it possible that large crowds of people could be running in mass confusion to get away from these awful creatures and they simply don't have time or a means to even commit suicide? I think this is a possibility.

Verse 4 says that these creatures are attacking only those who do not have the seal of God in their foreheads, which would have to mean God is simply protecting those who are born-again and are trying to keep his commandments. It isn't wise at this point to be outside of God's family and his ark of protection. And it is especially not wise to be following the antichrist and his evil agenda. It will seem at the beginning that the antichrist has come as some kind of new savior and is ushering in a new utopia for mother earth, but it should be quite obvious to his followers by now that just the opposite is true. Nevertheless, they do not repent of their many and heinous sins.

Two More Woes

> One woe is past; and, behold, there come two woes hereafter. ... And the four angels were loosed, which were prepared for an hour, and a day, and a month, and a year, for to slay the third part of men. And the number of the army of the horsemen were two hundred thousand thousand: and I heard the number of them. And thus I saw the horses in the vision, and them that sat on them, having breastplates of fire, and of jacinth, and brimstone: and the heads of the horses were as the heads of lions; and out of their mouths issued fire and smoke and brimstone. (Rev. 9:12, 15–17)

I have always envisioned these horses that issue fire, smoke, and brimstone out of their mouths as tanks. Military tanks seem to fit the description quite well. They might be some kind of highly advanced tank of the future but with the same basic design in most ways. The second woe seems to be some sort of war that kills a third part of mankind, which should serve as a very terrible warning to those who remain, but let's look at what happens in the next verse.

> And the rest of the men which were not killed by these plagues yet repented not of the works of their hands, that they should not worship devils, and idols of gold, and silver, and brass, and stone, and of wood; which neither can see, nor hear, nor walk: Neither repented they of their murders, nor of their sorceries, nor of their fornication, nor of their thefts. (Rev. 9:20–21)

The third woe is the two witnesses. Revelation 11 describes them as the two olive trees or the two candlesticks standing before the God of the earth. These two witnesses are truly a mystery. Some commentators have said that they are Elijah and Moses brought back to fulfill this purpose. I tend to think, though, that God can do a new work and that these two figures are among the Hebrew population among the tribes.

Regardless of who they are, they stand before the very temple and defy the power of the antichrist to his face and in front of the rest of the world. If anyone tries to harm them, they are killed from fire that proceeds from their mouths. This may be real fire or symbolic of the Word of God. They also have power to keep it from raining and have the power to turn the waters to turn them to blood, as did Moses during the judgments on Egypt. The whole ministry of the two witnesses is obviously to show the unbelieving world—the world who has resisted the power of the Holy Spirit—that the power of God cannot be overcome under any circumstances. If the antichrist is able to defeat God, then why can't he defeat these two witnesses, who are obviously a terrible thorn in his side? But then God lifts his veil of protection, and they are overtaken.

> And when they shall have finished their testimony, the beast that ascendeth out of the bottomless pit shall overcome them, and kill them. (Rev. 11:7)

To the nonbeliever, this would appear to be a great victory. The two religious fanatics who tormented them and their leader are finally overcome by his own power. But it seems that God is trying to show the world that his hands of grace have lifted only for a brief moment, and it is within his perfect timing to bring these two witnesses home and to rest after their brief but powerful testimony and ministry for the Lord.

> And their dead bodies shall lie in the street of the great city, which spiritually is called Sodom and Egypt, where also our Lord was crucified. And they of the people and kindred's and tongues and nations shall see their dead bodies three days and a half, and shall not suffer their dead bodies to be put in graves. And they that dwell upon the earth shall rejoice over them, and make merry, and shall send gifts one to another, because these two prophets tormented them that dwelt on the earth. And after three days

> and a half the Spirit of life from God entered into
> them, and they stood upon their feet; and great
> fear fell upon them which saw them. And they
> heard a great voice from heaven saying unto
> them, come up hither. And they ascended up
> to heaven in a cloud; and their enemies beheld
> them. (Rev. 11:8–12)

It is very significant that God made it quite clear in these verses that the antichrist and all of his forces held no real power over life or death when it came to these two servants. As soon as the forces of evil had taken their lives, God called them to life again and resurrected them and brought them up to heaven in the very presence of his and their enemies. This, of course, is the truth and testimony to the world that God and God alone holds the keys to life and death, and there is no real victory except his own. They apparently missed the point again because there is no mention of a turnaround or repentance in any present or future passages. But I'm sure this will (in those days) serve as a great encouragement to the believers then living. It will definitely show that God is most certainly still on the throne, and no power in heaven or earth can change that fact.

Chapter 8

ARMAGEDDON

> And another angel came out of the temple,
> crying with a loud voice to him who sat on the
> cloud, "Thrust in your sickle and reap, for the
> time has come for you to reap, for the harvest if
> the earth is ripe. (Rev. 14:15)

There has been a terrible time of persecution for the true Christian believers of this great tribulation period. Thousands have died because they refuse to take the mark of the beast, and they refuse to go along with the hard-hearted one-world church that has arisen to a powerful status in the world. But the one-world church is finally destroyed, and the reign of the beast is almost over.

There is some detail given about Armageddon, such as Revelation 14:20: "And the winepress was trampled outside the city, and blood came out of the winepress, up to the horses bridles, for one thousand six hundred furlongs."

We are given here a picture of carnage so great that it reaches up to a horse's bridle. It's hard to imagine that this much blood could spill in one area and reach up that high. But the antichrist seems to have lost control of his dynasty. Revelation 16:16 says, "And he gathered them together into a place called in the Hebrew Armageddon."

The great armies of the world are finally amassed together to literally fight against the Lord of Hosts. After all the centuries, the world has never learned of the all-powerful presence of the Creator of all the universe. He cannot be defeated by ordinary means or conventional arms. He is ultra-dimensional and not of this world, but he rules over it.

These armies have gathered together in their own minds to fight against Israel. But underneath it all, it's to fight against God, who chose Israel for his own great purposes. It is in that day that God finally judges the unbelieving world for its stubborn and hard heart. The hardness of the consciousness says there is no reason to believe the Word of God because it is a book full of fantasies and fairytales. This hardness invented such deceptions such as evolution just to cover up the bright, shining, and unmistakable evidence of creation to prove God's existence once and for all. But no matter what evidence God brought forward, they ignored and denied it. They have also over the centuries denied the only begotten Son of glory sent to take upon himself the sins of the world. And not only have they denied him, but they have also now gathered together to see if they can wipe him out so they can continue to take pleasure in their own sin without being held accountable. But this is not going to happen.

> Therefore wait ye upon me, saith the Lord,
> until the day that rise up to the prey: For my
> determination is to gather the nations, that I
> may assemble the kingdoms to pour upon them
> mine indignation, even all my fierce anger: for
> all the earth shall be devoured with the fire of
> my jealousy. (Zeph. 3:8)

> Multitudes, multitudes in the valley of decision:
> for the day of the Lord is near in the valley of
> decision. (Joel 3:14)

The day has finally arrived that has brought both the armies of the Lord and the armies of Satan together to meet literally in the valley of Meggido. Satan has never really won a battle. The Lord won all of his battles of the past against all of Israel's foes. But apparently the Devil has never really learned his lesson and has to be taught this last one.

> I beheld till the thrones were cast down, and
> the Ancient of days did sit, whose garment was
> white as snow, and the hair of his head like
> the pure wool: his throne was like the fiery
> flame, and his wheels as burning fire. A fiery
> stream issued and came forth from before him:
> thousand thousands ministered unto him, and
> ten thousand stood before him: the judgment
> was set, and the books were opened. I beheld
> then because of the voice of the great words,

which the horn spake: I beheld even till the beast
was slain, and his body destroyed, and given to
the burning flame. (Dan. 7:9–11)

And in conclusion to God's book and mine:

His eyes were as a flame of fire, and on his head
were many crowns; and he had a name written,
that no man knew, but he himself. And he was
clothed with a vesture dipped in blood: and his
name is called the Word of God. And the armies
which were in heaven followed him upon white
horses, clothed in fine lined, white and clean.
And out of his mouth goeth a sharp sword, that
with it he should smite the nations: and he shall
rule them with a rod of iron: and he treadeth
the winepress of the fierceness and wrath of
Almighty God. And he hath on his vesture and on
his thigh a name written, KING OF KINGS, AND
LORD OF LORDS. ... And the beast was taken, and
with him the false prophet that wrought miracles
before him, with which he deceived them that
had received the mark of the beast and them that
worshipped his image. These both were cast alive
into a lake of fire burning with brimstone. And
the remnant were slain with the sword of him
that sat upon the horse, which sword proceeded
out of his mouth: and all the fowls were filled
with their flesh. (Rev. 19:12–16, 20–21)

Jesus said in Matthew 24 that he would return in the clouds with great power and great glory. He returns to earth during the battle of Armageddon, stops the battle, and sets up his kingdom. The antichrist and his worldly system are completely destroyed, and the earth is restored to a beautiful, sinless world, as it was meant to be in the beginning.

Yes, the world has to go through this time of terrible tribulation and trouble like has never been seen before. But in the end, it is all set right again, and every knee shall bow and every tongue confess that he is truly King of Kings and Lord of Lords.

SUGGESTED READING LIST

Baaker, Jim. *I Was Wrong*. Nashville, TN: Thomas Nelson, 1997.

_____. *Prosperity and the Coming Apocalypse*. Nashville, TN: Thomas Nelson, 1998.

Bernall, Misty. *She Said Yes: The Unlikely Martyrdom of Cassie Bernall*. New York: Pocket Books, 1999.

Christopher, John. *The City of Gold and Lead*. New York: Simon Pulse, 2003.

_____. *The Pool of Lead and Fire*. New York: Simon Pulse, 2003.

_____. *The White Mountain*. New York: Simon Pulse, 2003.

Cruz, Nicky. *Run, Baby, Run*. City, State: Publisher, Year.

Decker, Ed. *The God Makers 1 and 2*. City, State: Publisher, Year.

Faid, Robert W. *A Scientific Approach to Biblical Mysteries*. City, State: Publisher, Year.

_____. *A Scientific Approach to Christianity*. City, State: Publisher, Year.

Foxe, John. *Foxe's Book of Martyrs*. City, State: Publisher, Year.

Hanegraaff, Hank. *Christianity in Crisis*. City, State: Publisher, Year. (This is also available as an audiobook and is highly recommended.)

_____. *Counterfeit Revival* (revised edition). City, State: Publisher, Year. (This is also available as an audiobook and is highly recommended.)

Hunt, Dave. *Occult Invasion*. City, State: Publisher, Year.

_____. *The Seduction of Christianity.* City, State: Publisher, Year. (I also recommend Dave Hunt's newsletter.)

Kreeft, Peter and Tacelli, Robert K. *Handbook of Christian Apologetics.* City, State: Publisher, Year.

L'Engle, Madeline. *A Wrinkle in Time.* City, State: Publisher, Year.

Little, Paul E. *Know What You Believe.* City, State: Publisher, Year.

_____. *Know Why You Believe.* City, State: Publisher, Year.

MacArthur, John. *Charismatic Chaos.* City, State: Publisher, Year.

Martin, Walter. *Kingdom of the Cults.* City, State: Publisher, Year.

McConnell, D. R. *A Different Gospel.* City, State: Publisher, Year.

McDowell, Josh. *The New Evidence that Demands a Verdict.* City, State: Publisher, Year.

Nimmo, Beth, Scott, Darrell, and Rabey, Steve. *Rachel's Tears: The Spiritual Journey of Columbine Martyr Rachel Scott.* City, State: Publisher, Year.

Packer, J. I. *Hot Tub Religion.* City, State: Publisher, Year.

Randies, Bill. *Beware of the New Prophets.* City, State: Publisher, Year.

Sire, James W. *The Universe Next Door.* City, State: Publisher, Year.

Strobel, Lee. *The Case for a Creator.* City, State: Publisher, Year.

_____. *The Case for Christ.* City, State: Publisher, Year.

_____. *The Case for Faith.* City, State: Publisher, Year.

Wilkerson, David. *The Cross and the Switchblade.* City, State: Publisher, Year.

_____. *The Vision.* City, State: Publisher, Year.

Wurmbrand, Richard. *Tortured for Christ.* City, State: Publisher, Year.